Mridula Baljekar,

a leading Indian cookbook writer and broadcaster,
has written several books, including the best-selling
Complete Indian Cookbook, *Quick Vegetarian Curries*,
and *Real Fast Indian Food*. She lives in England.

Indian Cooking Without Fat

Indian Cooking Without Fat

The Revolutionary New Way
to Enjoy Healthy and
Delicious Indian Food

Mridula Baljekar

Marlowe & Company
New York

INDIAN COOKING WITHOUT FAT:
The Revolutionary New Way to Enjoy Healthy and Delicious Indian Food
Copyright © 1999, 2001 by Mridula Baljekar
Photographs by Ken Field

Published by
Marlowe & Company
An Imprint of Avalon Publishing Group Incorporated
161 William Street, 16th Floor
New York, NY 10038

Originally published in the UK by Metro Books, an imprint of
Metro Publishing Limited. This edition published by arrangement.

The publisher would like to thank Linda Rao for her
editorial contributions to the American edition.

Library of Congress Cataloging-in-Publication Data is available for this title.
ISBN 1-56924-545-2

9   8   7   6   5   4   3   2   1

Designed by Pauline Neuwirth, Neuwirth & Associates, Inc.

Printed in the United States of America
Distributed by Publishers Group West

This book is dedicated to all those who believe that
healthy eating is a way of life and that *no fat*
doesn't necessarily mean *no taste*!

Contents

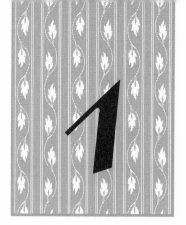

Introduction

WHEN YOU THINK OF Indian food do you have visions of meat and vegetables floating in a sea of oil? Do you sometimes wish it wasn't so oily and that you could eat it more often? Now there is a way.

My revolutionary cooking method will give you the chance to enjoy delicious Indian meals, packed with flavor and nutritious ingredients, but without significant quantities of added fat!

The majority of the recipes have the right type of fat in minimum quantities, and in many cases oil isn't added at all. These unique dishes will not only give you great taste but will also guard your health.

I'm not suggesting that you exclude fat altogether from your diet. Indeed, some fat is essential to the body. Fat enhances the flavor of any food, not just Indian cuisine. Fat is also an important nutrient and a high source of energy and carries fat-soluble vitamins. Fats and oils help enhance the characteristic aroma, taste, and texture of most food. It is knowing which type of fat to include and which to avoid, or to consume in small quantities, that is the first and most important step in following a healthy diet.

There are three crucial types of fats that affect our diet. These are: **saturates** (present mainly in animal fats, but also in coconut and palm oil); **monounsaturates** (found mainly in olive oil, and also in rapeseed, nut and seed oils); **polyunsaturates** (found in vegetable, nut and seed oils, as well as in oily fish such as mackerel, sardines, salmon, and herring).

According to experts, we don't really need saturated fat in our diet. In fact, eating too much of this type of fat can cause high blood cholesterol, which can lead to heart disease and some forms of cancer. Reducing saturates in our diet is essential to maintaining a healthy lifestyle.

By reducing or avoiding saturates, we automatically reduce the energy supply to our body. But we can close this gap easily by using more of the two beneficial types of fats: monounsaturates and polyunsaturates (including omega-3 fatty acids), which are believed to be beneficial to the heart.

In traditional Indian cooking, however, saturated fat plays a major role. Oil or ghee (clarified butter) is used to fry onions and spices. And I must admit that, very often, people use a lot more of these fats than they need to. Frying the spices before adding the main ingredient is the very essence of Indian cooking. Spices need to be fried gently to enhance their flavors and achieve the desired taste and texture. But it isn't always necessary to fry the spices in oil or ghee. Nor is it necessary to do this at the beginning of the cooking process. This can also be done *without any added fat in the middle or at the end of the process*.

Invisible Fat

Everyone is aware of "invisible fat," or the fat that's naturally present in certain types of food. One day, during a frantic rush to get the family meal ready, I discovered that I could use this natural fat to fry the spices and produce delicious Indian dishes without any added fat. What led to this discovery? I had to use up some marinated lamb, which had sat in my fridge for 36 hours. I put the lamb in a heavy saucepan and just let it stew in its own juices until it was almost tender. I then dried off all the natural juices by leaving the pan uncovered and, when it was completely dry, I browned the meat in its own fat, cooking the spices at the same time! A hint of coconut milk (it is very high in fat, so only a dash) and fresh cilantro to finish off the dish produced one of the most delicious lamb curries I had ever tasted, and my family agreed.

In my excitement, I embarked on a long process of testing Indian recipes using the minimum of fat, and this book is the result.

The Importance of Heat

I always loved watching my mother and grandmother creating wonderful-looking and delicious dishes. Once, when I was about ten years old, I remember my mother telling me that what the spices really needed to enhance their flavors was *heat*. Gentle heat activates the volatile oils in the spices and greatly enhances their flavor. The important factor is the correct level of heat. Too much heat will dry out the essential oils and ruin the flavor; too little will do nothing to enhance them. This made more sense to me when, later on, I saw how my mother-in-law gently roasted the whole spices before grinding them. She added the roasted and ground spices to her chosen dish without frying them again. She would then add a hot oil seasoning to finish the dish.

The Absence of Fat

The process of dry roasting the spices is quite quick and simple. These dishes were very low in fat as they consisted mainly of vegetables, legumes, beans, and lentils. In most of my recipes I have used this technique, but have omitted the hot oil seasoning in the meat and poultry dishes (there is enough natural fat in meat and poultry), and the dishes turned out very well. This further convinced me that adding extra fat was quite unnecessary.

The absence of natural fat, however, makes it difficult to cook vegetables, lentils, beans, and certain types of fish without sacrificing the flavor. To overcome this, I have used small quantities of polyunsaturated fat—such as sunflower or canola oil—in all these recipes.

With a little care and imagination, and a lot of patience, I have achieved authentic flavors in both newly created and traditional recipes. Indian food is generally very healthy because the dishes are full of fresh vegetables, beans, legumes, and whole wheat flour for the everyday bread (chapatis). Combine these nutritious ingredients with meat, fish, and poultry dishes with no added fat and you have a winning formula for a healthy lifestyle.

There is one important point that I would like you to remember when using this book: by added fat I mean mainly *saturated fat*. Certain types of fat are actually beneficial to our health. I have not excluded the following items as they're perfectly safe as long as we consume them in moderation.

Nuts: All types of nuts are good sources of protein and vitamin E. They're also a high source of fat, but it is a "good" fat, so can be used in small quantities.

Seeds: Sesame and poppy seeds are also high in fat but only small quantities are required. They're great flavor enhancers and are an essential part of Indian cooking. They help thicken the sauces, too. Sunflower seeds are a good source of fiber and lend a wonderfully nutty taste to a sauce.

Dairy Products: Reduced-fat alternatives such as skim or 2% milk, fat-free half-and-half, low-fat yogurt, modified low-fat plain yogurt, low-fat sour cream, and paneer (Indian cheese) are all acceptable in moderation.

Coconut: This has a high fat content, so I have used desiccated (dry) coconut sparingly in a few recipes for the sake of taste and authentic flavor. I have avoided creamed coconut except for one recipe (see Lamb in Coconut Milk, page 126). This was my first prototype recipe that launched the entire concept of cooking Indian food without added fat.

My Methods for Great Flavors

1. You can use pre-cooked onion purée instead of fat to fry spices.
2. Pre-roasted ground spices are used in the majority of the recipes, which add loads of flavor, but no fat.

3. Tandoori dishes are low-fat in any case, but I have further reduced the fat by not using oil or butter for basting, as is usually done. They taste delicious with my fat-free basting sauces.

4. I have adapted traditional deep-fried dishes for grilling or baking with a light brushing of oil for fabulous results.

Some Hints

There are a few important points to remember before you embark on this revolutionary cooking method:

1. You do need to invest in a couple of good quality nonstick saucepans. A nonstick surface is safer for Indian cooking methods, because you will be able to cook the spices without them sticking to the pan. When the spices stick to the pan, they can burn quickly, spoiling the flavor completely. A nonstick pan also allows you to use as little oil as possible.

2. Because oil-free cooking is designed for a healthy lifestyle, it is also a good idea to choose the food you want to cook with care. The following items are listed in ascending order of fat content:

   → fish (1% in general. Oily fish, such as mackerel, have more of the polyun-saturates, which are beneficial)
   → skinned chicken breast (4% fat)
   → pork (4% fat)
   → beef (4.6% fat)
   → lamb (8.8% fat)

3. In Indian dishes, poultry is always skinned, and excess fat is removed from both meat and poultry before cooking. This method is even more important in fat-free cooking. Always remove the skin from chicken, because the skin contains the greatest amount of fat. Also remove as much visible fat as you can from all meat and poultry. You'll still find just enough fat oozing out of them to fry the spices.

4. It's a good idea to refrigerate marinating meat when possible, but it must be brought back to room temperature before cooking, which, depending on the quantity, takes between thirty minutes and an hour.

About Salt

Salt plays an important role in achieving a balanced spice flavor in Indian cuisine. It's important to consider the type of food to which the salt is added and whether you need to add extra salt to the dish at the table.

Only raw fish, poultry, and meat, which have no added salt (unlike ham or bacon), are used in Indian cooking. Because we achieve a well-rounded flavor with the right amount of spices and salt during cooking, it's usually unnecessary to add salt to an Indian meal at the table. Instead of stock cubes, Indian cooking makes use of homemade, highly aromatic stocks with no added salt.

In all the recipes, I have used the right amount of salt needed to create a balanced flavor. If the level of salt still seems high to you compared to Western cooking, and if it is enough to worry you, then by all means adjust it to your liking. It is the sodium that causes the problem. There are low-sodium versions of salt available in most supermarkets; you could use one of these as an alternative.

Weight Loss and Healthy Eating

Although you will certainly benefit from a low-fat diet, I do not claim that this book is the answer to a dieter's dream. By ensuring that no added fat is used in the recipes, you have taken the first and foremost step to following a healthy diet. This book is also not a manual for healthy eating, but you can safely use it as a guide. To help you, each recipe is accompanied by a nutritional analysis telling you how many calories, how many grams of fat, and how many grams of saturated fat each serving contains. (The saturated fat is part of the total amount of fat, not in addition to it.) Where a recipe provides a range of portions (for example, serves 4 to 5), the analysis is for the smaller number of portions (that is, in this example, 4, not 5).

My aim is to give you the chance to enjoy Indian food without having to worry about consuming too much fat. The link between fat and calories is clear: Since fat contains more calories per gram than either carbohydrate or protein, cutting your fat intake must be your first step in developing a healthy eating routine. And, as this book will demonstrate, if the fat that's naturally present in food is enough to enhance the flavors of spices, why add more?

Happy cooking! Eat well! Live well!

A Guide to Ingredients

THE FOLLOWING IS A list of some of the ingredients used in this book. If you are unsure about how to buy or store certain ingredients, this list, together with the Cook's Tips included throughout, should help.

Aniseed (Ajowain or Carum) Anise is native to India. The seed resembles a celery seed and is related to caraway and cumin, though the flavor is more akin to thyme. All Indian grocers sell anise and the seeds, which are used with legumes and fried snacks, will keep for a number of years if you store them in an airtight container. Anise aids digestion and helps to prevent flatulence.

Chapati flour (Atta) This very fine whole wheat flour, used to make all unleavened Indian bread, is rich in dietary fiber because, unlike whole wheat flour, atta is made by grinding the whole grain into a very fine powder.

Bay leaf (Tej patta) Bay leaves used in Indian cooking are obtained from the cassia tree and are quite different from Western bay leaves (from the sweet bay laurel). Because Indian bay leaves aren't readily available, you can use standard bay leaves instead.

Black peppercorns (Kali mirchi) Black pepper comes from allowing fresh green berries to dry in the sun. The green berries come from the pepper vine native to monsoon forests of southwest India. Whole peppercorns will keep well in an airtight jar but ground black pepper loses its wonderful aromatic flavor very quickly. It is best to keep a supply of whole pepper in a mill and grind it only when you need to use it. Pepper is believed to be a good remedy for flatulence.

⊰Cardamom (Elaichi)⊱ Cardamom has been used in Indian cooking since ancient times. Southern India produces an abundance of cardamom and it is from there that this spice found its way to Europe via the ancient spice route.

There are two types of cardamom: the small green cardamoms (*choti elaichi*) and the big dark brown cardamoms, which are generally referred to as black cardamoms. In the West, we also see a third variety, white cardamoms, which are obtained by blanching small green cardamoms. The blanching produces a milder flavor.

Whole green cardamom pods are used to flavor rice and different sauces. You can buy ground cardamom, which is used in many desserts and drinks, at Indian stores. It's best, however, to grind small quantities at home using a coffee or spice mill. If this spice is stored for too long, the essential natural oils will dry out, which destroys the flavor. In India, cardamom seeds are chewed after a meal as a mouth freshener.

⊰Chaat masala⊱ Chaat masala (available from Indian or Pakistani stores) is a spice mix that you sprinkle on hot tandoori chicken. Although adding it to the recipe is optional, it's worth trying, because it transforms the flavor dramatically.

⊰Chilies (Mirchi)⊱ It is difficult to judge the strength of chilies. Generally, the small, thin chilies are hot and the large fleshy ones tend to be milder. Most of the heat comes from the seeds, so it is best to remove them if you don't enjoy hot food. You can remove the seeds in two ways. First, you can halve the chili lengthwise, then scrape out the seeds under running water using a small knife. The second technique is to roll the chili between the palms of your hands for a few seconds, which loosens the seeds. Then you slit the chili (without cutting it through completely) and shake the seeds out.

Always wash your hands thoroughly after handling chilies, as their juices are a severe irritant, particularly to eyes or tender areas of skin. To remove all traces of pungency, rub a little oil into your hands, then rub in lemon juice.

Fresh green chilies: These long, slim fresh green chilies are sold in Indian stores. Chilies that come from the Canary Islands tend to be milder than Indian chilies. Jalapeño and serrano chilies from Mexico are more readily available in supermarkets—they aren't ideal for Indian cooking, but you can use them.

Fresh red chilies: Mainly from Thailand, these are sold in most large supermarkets.

Dried red chilies (Lal mirchi): When fresh green chilies are ripe, they turn a rich red color. When these peppers are dried to produce dried red chilies, they develop a completely different flavor. You can't use fresh chilies instead of dried, nor can you use dried rather than fresh. Crushed dried chilies are coarsely ground and are sold in Indian and Pakistani shops; you can also prepare them at home in a coffee or spice mill. Supermarkets also sell crushed dried red chilies, which are also ground into chili powder.

Bird's eye chilies: These small, pointed and extremely hot peppers are normally used whole to flavor oil. Long slim chilies are weaker and are ground with other spices.

⋇ Cilantro, fresh ⋇
Cooks use this herb, which is really the fresh leaves of the coriander plant, in Indian cooking for flavor as well as a garnish. Cilantro also forms the basis for many chutneys and pastes.

⋇ Cinnamon (Dalchini) ⋇
One of the oldest spices, cinnamon is obtained from the dried bark of a tropical plant related to the laurel family. It gives savory and sweet dishes a warm flavor.

⋇ Cloves (Lavang) ⋇
Cloves are the unripened buds of a south Asian evergreen tree. They have a distinctive flavor and are used both whole and ground. In India, cloves are used as a breath freshener. Clove oil is used to ease toothache.

⋇ Coconut (Nariyal) ⋇
Coconut palms grow in abundance in southern India and fresh coconut is used in savory and sweet dishes. Alternatives to fresh coconut include desiccated and creamed varieties. If you use desiccated coconut or coconut milk, make sure that it is unsweetened. Coconut is high in saturated fat; however, some grocery stores carry reduced-fat, canned coconut milk.

⋇ Coriander seeds (Dhaniya) ⋇
This is one of the most important spices in Indian cooking. Its sweet, mellow flavor blends well with vegetables.

⋇ Cumin (Jeera) ⋇
This pungent spice can be used whole or ground. Be sure to always measure the quantity of this spice because it has a strong flavor. The seeds are used whole to flavor cooking oil before the vegetables are added to the recipe. You can obtain a more rounded flavor if the seeds are roasted, then ground.

There are two varieties, black (*kala jeera*) and white (*safed jeera*), each with its own distinctive flavor, and the two aren't interchangeable. Black cumin is sometimes confused with caraway.

⋇ Curry leaves (Kari patta) ⋇
Grown and used extensively all over southern India, these leaves have an assertive flavor and are used with vegetables and legumes. They're sold fresh or dried in Indian grocery stores. You can store the dried leaves in an airtight jar, but you can freeze the fresh leaves—which have a better flavor—to add to dishes when you need them.

⊰ Fennel (Saunf) ⊱   These green-yellow seeds are slightly larger than cumin and have a flavor similar to anise. They have been used in Indian cooking since ancient times and they're also chewed as a breath freshener or to settle an upset stomach.

⊰ Garam Masala ⊱   *Garam* means heat and *masala* is the blending of different spices. The main ingredients in this spice mix are cinnamon or cassia, cloves, and black pepper, with other spices according to individual taste. These main ingredients are believed to create body heat and are used to make a warming spiced tea in extreme climates in the Himalayan region. To learn more about garam masala, see page 23.

⊰ Garlic (Lasoon) ⊱   Fresh garlic is indispensable in Indian cooking. Dried flakes, powder, and garlic salt just can't offer the same authentic flavor. Garlic is always used crushed or puréed to yield the maximum flavor. This bulb is believed to be beneficial in reducing blood cholesterol levels; it also has antiseptic properties and aids digestion.

⊰ Ginger (Adrak) ⊱   With its fresh, but warm and woody flavor, fresh ginger is vital to Indian cooking. Dried (powdered) ginger can't give the same fresh flavor. Ginger is believed to reduce stomach acidity and promote good blood circulation.

⊰ Gram flour or chickpea flour (Besan) ⊱   Made from ground chickpeas, these flours are available at Indian grocery stores.

⊰ Mint (Pudina) ⊱   Native to the Mediterranean and West Asian countries, mint is easy to grow and readily available. Dried mint is a good substitute in Indian cooking.

⊰ Modified low-fat plain yogurt ⊱   Instead of Greek-strained yogurt, which can be hard to find, I have used modified low-fat plain yogurt in several of the recipes in this book. Here's how to make it: Strain low-fat plain yogurt through a muslin-lined sieve over a bowl to remove excess moisture. This will take 25 to 30 minutes. Remember: You'll need double the quantity of yogurt because it reduces considerably by the time it is strained.

⊰ Moong dhal ⊱   These are skinned and split mung beans, and are available in Indian grocery stores.

⊰ Mustard (Sarsoon or Rai) ⊱   Mustard seeds are essential in Indian vegetarian cooking. Black and brown seeds, which have a nutty flavor, are most commonly used, and white seeds are reserved for pickles. You can also eat mustard leaves as a vegetable.

⊰ Nutmeg (Jaiphal) ⊱   Nutmeg has a hard, dark brown shell with a lacy covering. This covering is mace, the highly aromatic and brightly colored spice, which is removed from the nutmeg before the latter is sold. It's best to buy whole nutmegs, because the ready-ground spice loses its lovely aroma and flavor quickly. Use a small nutmeg grater for grating the whole nut.

Onion seeds (Kalonji) These tiny black seeds aren't true onion seeds; they've been given this name only because they bear a striking resemblance to onion seeds. These are used whole for flavoring fish, vegetables, pickles, and breads. Because there is really no substitute for onion seeds, it is best to leave them out of the recipe entirely if you're unable to find them.

Paneer Often referred to as cottage cheese in India, this is quite different from Western cottage cheese. Ricotta resembles paneer in flavor, but not in appearance, texture, or cooking qualities. Paneer is a firm, unripened, and unsalted cheese that doesn't melt and run like other cheeses when cooked, but withstands high temperatures to retain its shape. Paneer is available from larger supermarkets (sold pre-packed).

Paprika Hungary and Spain produce mild, sweet peppers that are dried and ground to make paprika. Deghi Mirchi is grown extensively in Kashmir for making Indian paprika: It's a mild spice that tints dishes a brilliant red without making them hot to eat. Hungarian paprika is the closest thing to Kashmiri Deghi Mirchi. If you'd like to add some "kick" to a dish that calls for paprika without hot chili powder, you can use two thirds paprika and one-third hot chili powder.

Poppy seeds (khus khus) The opium poppy produces the best seeds. There are two varieties, black or white, and only the white is used in Indian cooking. They're ground (sometimes roasted) and contribute a nutty flavor to sauces. They also act as a thickening agent.

Red lentils (Masoor dhal) You can buy these lentils at Indian grocery stores or in supermarkets.

Rose water This water contains the essence of an edible rose, the petals of which are used to garnish Mogul dishes. Dilute for use in savory and sweet dishes.

Rose-flavored syrup (rooh afza) This sweetener is available at Indian markets. You can use rose water instead, but the flavor is less concentrated and isn't sweetened.

Saffron (kesar) The saffron crocus grows extensively in Kashmir. Some 250,000 stamens are required to produce just slightly more than a pound of saffron. Only a minute quantity of this expensive, concentrated spice is required to flavor a dish.

≼ **Sesame seeds (til)** ≽ These are pale, creamy seeds with a rich nutty flavor. They're indigenous to India, which is the largest exporter of sesame oil to the West. Sprinkled on naan before baking, the seeds are also used with vegetables and in some sweet dishes. They're also used to thicken sauces.

≼ **Tamarind (imli)** ≽ Resembling pea pods at first, tamarind pods turn dark brown with a thin outer shell when ripe. The chocolate-brown flesh is encased in the shell, with seeds that have to be removed. The flesh is soaked in hot water to yield a pulp. Ready-to-use concentrated tamarind pulp is quick and easy to use. Valued for its distinctive tangy flavor, tamarind is added to vegetables, lentils and other legumes, and chutneys.

≼ **Toor dhal** ≽ These are yellow split lentils. They're available from Indian grocery stores.

≼ **Turmeric (haldi)** ≽ Fresh turmeric rhizomes resemble small pieces of ginger, with a beige-brown skin and bright yellow flesh. Fresh turmeric is dried and ground to produce the familiar spice, which has to be measured carefully to avoid giving dishes a bitter taste.

≼ **Whole wheat chapati flour (atta)** ≽ Available from Indian markets, you can store this flour the same way you would ordinary flour. A combination of whole wheat and white flour can be substituted (half and half) if this isn't available.

≼ **Yellow split peas (channa dhal)** ≽ These legumes are available in supermarkets or in large bags from Indian markets.

≼ **Yogurt (dahi)** ≽ In India yogurt is always homemade, and usually from buffalo milk, which is creamier than cow's milk. Indian yogurt is also mild. Throughout the recipes, low-fat plain yogurt is listed as an ingredient.

A Well-Stocked Cupboard

INDIAN COOKING IS enjoyable when you have a well-stocked cupboard. It is worth making a trip to a good Indian grocery store to stock up on ingredients. These are ingredients I always keep in stock.

Spices

Keep a supply of all the spices and seeds already listed, storing them in airtight jars, away from direct light. As well as whole spices, have the following ground spices: coriander, chili powder, cumin, garam masala (bought or homemade, see pages 10 and 23), paprika, and turmeric. Curry leaves and bay leaves can be dried or the fresh leaves can be frozen.

Dry Ingredients

Apart from the usual dry ingredients readily available from all supermarkets, dhal, besan (gram or chickpea flour), and chapati flour are useful for Indian cooking. Basmati rice is, of course, essential.

Canned Food

Chopped tomatoes are fairly standard cupboard items, and legumes are versatile: chickpeas, butter beans, and kidney beans are used in this book. Although not a canned food, tomato purée is another item to keep in stock (a tube is more convenient than a can).

Standard Fresh Ingredients

Onions are, of course, essential in every kitchen for the majority of savory cooking. Garlic, ginger, and chilies are also crucial for Indian cooking. Store garlic and ginger in a cool dry place, preferably with potatoes. Remove the stalks from fresh green chilies, then store them in an airtight jar in the refrigerator for 3 to 4 weeks. (They can also be frozen.) Onion, garlic, and ginger can also be made into purées and chilled or frozen (see Basic Recipes on pages 16–18).

Cilantro, bought in a bunch with roots intact, can be stored in a jug of water for 6 to 7 days if you change the water daily. Alternatively, wrap the roots with damp kitchen paper and tie the bunch in a large plastic bag, then store the herb in the salad drawer of the refrigerator. Tie the bag loosely, forcing out extra air, and store it with the roots down. Alternatively, chopped cilantro freezes well and is ready for immediate use.

Specialty Items

Tamarind concentrate or juice and rose-flavored syrup (*rooh afza*) are delicious ingredients in some of these recipes. Reduced-fat coconut milk is available from larger supermarkets and health food stores.

Basic Recipes

FAT MAKES FOOD TASTY—that's why we like it so much. These basic preparations replace and enhance flavors that may be diminished by reducing or omitting fat from recipes. They also make Indian cooking simpler and speedier. Many of the items in this chapter can be bought prepared, but the homemade version is vastly superior in flavor and aroma.

In a modern kitchen, a coffee or spice mill, blender and food processor replace the traditional grinding stone. A coffee mill is used to prepare many ingredients in this book and a blender and/or food processor is also used throughout.

Roasting Spices

Spices are roasted in a dry pan. A cast-iron or heavy frying pan or small saucepan is best. A heavy pan retains heat after the heat source has been turned off and roasts spices evenly. Throughout the recipes, where ingredients are dry roasted, use a heavy pan; if you have only thin cookware, take care to regulate the heat because the ingredients burn more easily.

Be sure to roast the spices at the correct temperature and for the times specified. Under- or overcooking the spices will not improve their flavors; in fact, if overcooked, some essential oils in the spices are lost, resulting in less flavor.

Remove the spices from the pan immediately to prevent further cooking, and spread them out on a plate. Leave to cool for about 5 minutes before grinding.

Garlic Purée

SERVINGS: Makes 1 lb., 2 oz.
PREPARATION TIME: 30 minutes

Garlic is used in most Indian dishes, except for those cooked on religious occasions. This is because it is considered to be a stimulant, not to be consumed on days when the mind should be void of all temptation. Preparing fresh garlic for each recipe can be time-consuming, but it is easy to make a batch of garlic purée and store it in the refrigerator or freezer. When buying garlic, look for firm, plump and unbroken bulbs. Fresh bulbs, tinged with pink, are juicy, delicious, and full of essential oils. Store garlic at room temperature, ideally in a cool, dry place.

8–10	garlic bulbs, about 1 lb., peeled
1/4 teaspoon	citric acid (optional)

→ To peel the garlic, first lightly crush the cloves with gentle pressure to loosen the skin. The back of a wooden spoon or a large knife can be used for this. Remove the skins.

→ Purée the garlic in a blender with 5 fl. oz. water. Store the garlic purée in an airtight container in the refrigerator. It will keep for up to 15 days; it may discolor slightly, but this will not affect the flavor. If you are worried about the garlic discoloring, add the citric acid when puréeing the garlic.

→ Freeze garlic purée in small airtight freezer containers, placing them in a sealed plastic bag to prevent the garlic odor from tainting other foods in the freezer. Freeze for up to 6 months.

COOK'S TIP: When preparing 1–2 garlic cloves for a recipe, it is easier to leave the cloves whole (even though this makes peeling them slightly more difficult) and then either grate them on the fine blade of a grater or crush them with a little salt to make a smooth pulp. For 1 teaspoon smooth purée, use 1 large or 2 medium garlic cloves.

Healthy Hint

In India, garlic has been used for thousands of years to cure ailments such as bronchitis, asthma, colds, and coughs. It has also been used in ritual healing. Modern research suggests that garlic may help to lower blood cholesterol and inhibit blood clots.

Ginger Purée

SERVINGS: Makes 1 lb.
PREPARATION TIME: 10–15 minutes

Along with onion and garlic, ginger is one of the three ingredients that make up the well-known "wet trinity" used in Indian cooking. When buying ginger, look for a piece that feels firm and has thin, shiny skin. Store ginger in a cool, dry place, away from direct light. Unless grated or puréed, ginger doesn't keep well in the refrigerator. Ideally, store it with potatoes for best results. Prepared ginger sold in jars or tubes doesn't have the same flavor as this homemade purée.

1 lb.	fresh ginger, peeled and coarsely chopped

→ Purée the ginger with 5 fl. oz. water in a blender until smooth. Mature ginger is fibrous and requires slightly longer blending than young roots. Continue blending until you achieve a smooth texture.

→ Store the ginger purée in an airtight container in the refrigerator. It will keep for up to 15 days. Alternatively, freeze the purée in small, airtight freezer containers. Freeze for up to 6 months.

COOK'S TIP: It is easier to use a vegetable peeler than a knife to peel ginger and you do not lose any of the flesh. Instead of puréeing ginger, it can be grated on a fairly fine blade of a grater (but not the finest, as the ginger will stick to it). For 1 teaspoon finely grated ginger, use a 1-inch cube of fresh ginger.

Healthy Hint

Ginger was used by ancient Chinese and Indian herbalists
as a cure for acidity, nausea, and poor circulation.
Fresh ginger juice mixed with honey is still
given as a cure for a dry, tickly cough.

Boiled Onion Purée

SERVINGS: Makes 1¾ lbs.
PREPARATION TIME: 10 minutes
COOKING TIME: 15 minutes

Onions are cooked in different ways to achieve the characteristic textures and flavors of individual dishes. Boiled onion purée is commonly used to thicken sauces, adding its own distinctive flavor when cooked with spices. Even though I have not used large quantities of fat for frying onions and spices in the recipes, I am amazed at the fantastic flavors produced by these traditional ingredients when they're combined with the modest amount of fat naturally present in meat and poultry.

1 lb., 10 oz.	onions, coarsely chopped
6	green cardamom pods, bruised

➔ Place the onions and cardamoms in a saucepan. Pour in 2 cups water and bring to a boil. Reduce the heat to medium, cover and cook for 15 minutes, or until the onions are soft. Set aside to cool.

➔ Remove the cardamom pods and purée the onions with their cooking liquid in a blender. Store in an airtight container in the refrigerator for 8–10 days. Alternatively, pack in 8 oz. portions in airtight containers and freeze for up to 6 months.

Browned Sliced Onions

SERVINGS: Makes 6–8 oz.
PREPARATION TIME: 5 minutes
COOKING TIME: 10–15 minutes

*F*ried onions are a popular, appetizing garnish for many Indian dishes, particularly rice dishes, such as pilaus and biryanis. Add a special touch to plain boiled rice by topping it with a little fried onion. Try this low-fat version of fried onions—the quantity given is enough to garnish at least two dishes.

2	large onions, peeled, halved, and finely sliced
1/4 teaspoon	sugar
3/4 teaspoon	salt
2 teaspoons	sunflower or canola oil

→ Place the onions in a nonstick frying pan with the remaining ingredients and cook over medium heat for 3–4 minutes.

→ Add 3 tablespoons water and continue to cook for an additional 3–4 minutes, until the onions begin to brown.

→ Pour in 2½ fl. oz. water and cook for 4–5 minutes, until the onions are soft and the water has evaporated. Continue to cook for another 1–2 minutes, if necessary, until the onions are well browned. Remove from the heat and use as required. The onions can be stored in a covered container in the refrigerator for 4–5 days.

COOK'S TIP: A large quantity of onions can be prepared and frozen. Pack them in airtight containers and freeze for up to 6 months.

Browned Onion Purée

SERVINGS: Makes 11 oz.
PREPARATION TIME: 15 minutes
COOKING TIME: about 30 minutes

*I*n their traditional dishes, north Indian chefs fry the onions until well browned, then purée them. This creates a wonderful flavor and thickens sauces at the same time. To achieve this without fat, I have browned the onions with a little salt and sugar by cooking them slowly until the sugar caramelizes.

2 lbs.	onions, finely sliced
1 teaspoon	salt
1 tablespoon	sugar

→ Mix the ingredients in a saucepan and stir over low heat. When the onions begin to sizzle, sprinkle in 1 tablespoon water, stir well, and cover the pan. Cook for 15 minutes, by which time the onions will have released all their natural moisture.

→ Increase the heat to medium and cook, uncovered and stirring frequently, for an additional 12–15 minutes or until the liquid has evaporated.

→ Remove from the heat and set aside to cool slightly. Process the onions until smooth in a food processor or blender, or press them through a sieve. Use as required.

→ The purée can be stored in an airtight container in the refrigerator for up to 15 days. Alternatively, make a large quantity and freeze it in 8 oz. batches, which is the average quantity used in a recipe. The purée can be frozen for up to 6 months.

Healthy Hint

Onions may help to reduce high blood cholesterol and reduce
the risk of coronary heart disease. Like garlic, they're
believed to contain a compound that helps to prevent the
blood from clotting and may increase the rate at which clots
are broken down. They also contain sulfur compounds,
which may help to prevent the growth of cancer cells.

Ground Roasted Cumin

SERVINGS: Makes 8 oz.
PREPARATION TIME: 5 minutes
COOKING TIME: 3 minutes

*R*oasting and grinding spices not only enhances their flavor, but it also prolongs their shelf life. Using ground roasted spices more than compensates for any absence of fat.

8 oz.	cumin seeds

→ Preheat a cast-iron or heavy frying pan over medium heat for 2 minutes. Reduce the heat to very low and add the cumin seeds. Stir them continuously for about 1 minute, when the seeds will release their aroma. Remove from the heat and tip the seeds out onto a large plate to prevent further cooking. Leave to cool.

→ Grind the cumin to a powder in a coffee mill. Store in an airtight jar away from direct light. This will preserve the warm flavor and aroma of the ground cumin for 10–12 weeks.

Healthy Hint

In India the curative properties of cumin have been known since ancient times. It is believed to be an effective remedy for stomach disorders, such as indigestion, diarrhea, and flatulence. Roasted and ground cumin is added to hot water and blended with honey, then taken as a cure for colds and the associated aches and pains.

Ground Roasted Coriander

SERVINGS: Makes 8 oz.
PREPARATION TIME: 5 minutes
COOKING TIME: 3 minutes

Coriander is used in Indian cooking almost every day, either in the form of the dried spice or as the fresh leaves, and it controls the basic flavors of all Indian dishes. Roasting not only enhances the flavors of the spice, it also makes it easier to grind. Roasted ground coriander retains its peak flavor and aroma for many weeks and is sufficiently mellow to complement almost any food. For instant flavor, sprinkle this spice over plain grilled or roasted fish, poultry, or meat.

8 oz.   coriander seeds

→ Preheat a cast-iron or heavy frying pan over medium heat for 2 minutes. Reduce the heat to very low and add the coriander seeds. Stir them continuously for about 1 minute, when the seeds will release their aroma. Remove from the heat and tip the seeds out on to a large plate to prevent further cooking. Leave to cool.

→ Grind the coriander to a powder in a coffee or spice mill. Store in an airtight jar away from direct light. This will preserve the warm flavor and aroma of the ground coriander for 10–12 weeks.

Healthy Hint

Fresh cilantro, the leaves of the coriander plant, is used not only to garnish, but also to flavor dishes: for example, salads, chutneys, and relishes. Although in prepared dishes coriander is eaten in such small quantities that it doesn't make a significant contribution to the diet, the juice extracted from fresh cilantro leaves by pounding or puréeing is rich in vitamins and iron. Coriander seeds are infused in hot water and used as a remedy for digestive disorders and urinary problems.

Garam Masala

SERVINGS: Makes 4½ oz.
PREPARATION TIME: 15 minutes
COOKING TIME: 2 minutes

Garam masala is that magic ingredient that instantly transforms an Indian dish with its special zest and warmth. There are many good-quality brands of garam masala that you can use, but I had to share my family recipe with you as I have not found a bought version that can beat this for aroma and flavor. If you are short of time, you can enhance the flavor of bought garam masala by gently roasting it in a heavy pan over low heat for about 1 minute. Just follow your nose—as soon as you smell the aroma released by the spices, remove the pan from the heat and cool the garam masala immediately by spreading it out on a large plate or tray.

½ oz.	brown cardamom seeds (weight when removed from pods)
½ oz.	green cardamom seeds (weight when removed from pods)
1 oz.	cinnamon sticks, broken into small pieces
¼ oz.	cloves
¼ oz.	black peppercorns
2	whole nutmegs, about ½ oz., lightly crushed
½ oz.	coriander seeds
½ oz.	cumin seeds

→ Preheat a cast-iron or heavy frying pan over medium heat for 1 minute. Reduce the heat to low and add all the spices. Stir for about 1 minute, when the spices will begin to release their aroma. Remove from the heat and transfer to a plate or tray. Set aside to cool.

→ Grind the spices to a powder in a coffee or spice mill. Do this in batches and mix them together thoroughly when all the spices are ground. Store in an airtight jar away from direct light. Garam masala will stay fresh for about 12 weeks.

COOK'S TIP: Look for plump cardamom pods that aren't shrivelled. The seeds inside should be sticky, with a slight gloss. When buying black peppercorns, always look for larger berries as they have much more flavor. Both pepper and nutmeg lose their flavor quickly once ground, so buy them whole and store in airtight jars, away from direct light. To crush a whole nutmeg, place it in a plastic bag and hit it with a rolling pin.

Healthy Hint

Black pepper is believed to have diuretic and digestive properties. The volatile oil in nutmeg is an important ingredient in creams used to relieve rheumatic pains. Taken in measured quantities, it is also believed to cure insomnia and digestive problems.

Aromatic Stock

YAKHNI

SERVINGS: Makes 2¾ pints
PREPARATION TIME: 10 minutes
COOKING TIME: 1–1½ hours

*S*tock is widely used in the Muslim community in India, mainly in rich pilaus and biryanis, but also in some meat and poultry recipes. You can achieve a robust flavor without using stock in sauces by adding a few bones when you cook meat and poultry, but for rice dishes you do need a good stock. This stock is easy to make and it keeps well in the refrigerator. If you have to use bought stock, simmer it gently and briefly with the spices listed below, adding a little water to allow for evaporation.

1 lb., 2 oz.	chicken and lamb bones
3 3-inch	cinnamon sticks
10	cloves
10	green cardamom pods
1 teaspoon	black peppercorns
6	garlic cloves, unpeeled, lightly crushed
3-inch	cube of fresh ginger, unpeeled, sliced
1	large onion, unpeeled, quartered
1	parsnip, unpeeled, washed, and coarsely chopped
2–3	carrots, unpeeled, washed, and coarsely chopped

→ Place all the ingredients in a large saucepan and pour in 8 cups water. Bring to a boil, then reduce the heat to low, cover the pan and simmer for 1–1½ hours.

→ Strain the stock through a muslin-lined sieve. Pour into a heatproof container, cover and set aside to cool.

→ Place the stock in the refrigerator as soon as it is cool. It keeps well for more than a month. Boil the stock every 4–5 days, then return it to a clean container. Cover and cool the stock as quickly as possible, then return it to the refrigerator.

→ Alternatively, pour the stock into freezer containers, leaving headspace as it expands slightly on freezing, and freeze for up to 6 months.

Healthy Hint

As a home remedy, cinnamon infused in hot water brings relief to those suffering from the common cold. The volatile oil in cinnamon is believed to cure gastroenteritis and associated problems. It is also believed to aid digestion and help prevent nausea. Cardamom is believed to be helpful in reducing acidity and heartburn. This is, perhaps, the reason why cardamom pods coated with edible silver leaf are served after a meal in India. They act as a breath freshener and a digestive rolled into one. Cloves are highly antiseptic. In India, cloves are used as a remedy for bronchitis, and a clove is chewed to relieve toothache; they're also known to stimulate the digestive system. Together, these three spices are recognized for their ability to create body heat. To fight the bitter winter in the extreme north and the Himalayan region, tea laced with cinnamon, cardamom, and cloves is drunk every day.

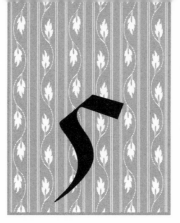

Snacks & Starters

WITHIN THE DIVERSITY of Indian cuisine there is an equally varied repertoire of snacks forming an important part of Indian culture. Relaxing over
delicious tidbits with a cup of tea or coffee is the normal way to end a hard
day's work and, when friends drop in, a plate of snacks is offered, irrespective of the time
of day or night. Children are given tasty morsels in their school lunch boxes, and there are
street vendors who display a variety of tantalizing snacks. When it comes to eating snacks,
we simply give in, tempted not only by the sight but also the air that is filled with the
aroma of delicious food.

Soups do not feature largely in Indian cooking and the tradition comes mainly from
the Mogul era. Spiced soups made from broth are generally served as a drink during a
meal. Western influence has changed this tradition to a certain extent, and I have created
the soups in this section to be served as a first course.

Starters, as in the Western sense, aren't a traditional part of an Indian meal. The dishes
I find served as starters in British restaurants are those that are eaten as snacks (or side
dishes) in India. Indian snacks are versatile. They're ideal with drinks or as side dishes;
they can also be served with a relish and bread to make a light lunch or supper. An Indian
meal doesn't consist of several courses. The dishes for the entire meal are served all at once,
and diners help themselves to what they want, in the order and quantity they prefer.

Vegetable Soup
Subzi ka Shorba

SERVINGS: 4
PREPARATION TIME: 15–20 minutes
COOKING TIME: 30 minutes
PER SERVING: Calories: 110; Fat: 3 g.; Saturated fat: 2 g.

This makes an ideal first course on its own or a light meal when served with bread and a relish such as Almond Chutney (see page 225).

1 lb.	potatoes, coarsely chopped
1–2	green chilies, seeded and chopped
1¼	teaspoons salt or to taste
2 teaspoons	Ginger Purée (see page 17)
1 teaspoon	Garlic Purée (see page 16)
8 oz.	white mushrooms, finely chopped
1 teaspoon	paprika
2	scallions, white part only, finely chopped
1 tablespoon	finely chopped fresh cilantro leaves
2 tablespoons	fat-free half-and-half

→ Put the potatoes, chilies, and salt in a saucepan and add 15 fl. oz. water. Bring to a boil, reduce the heat to medium, and cover the pan. Cook for 12–15 minutes or until the potatoes are tender.

→ Mash the potatoes lightly in their cooking liquid and add an additional 10 fl. oz. water. Stir in the ginger and garlic purées, mushrooms, and paprika. Bring to a boil, cover, and reduce the heat to low. Simmer for 15 minutes.

→ Remove from the heat and stir in the scallions, cilantro, and half-and-half. Cover the pan and leave the soup to stand for 5 minutes before serving.

COOK'S TIP: If you'd like to make this dish a little spicier, you can use two-thirds paprika and one-third hot chili powder.

Zucchini Soup
Ghia ka Shorba

Servings: 4
Preparation time: 10 minutes, plus standing
Cooking time: 10–12 minutes
Per serving: Calories: 105; Fat: 7 g.; Saturated fat: 5 g.

This super-fast soup tastes delicious hot or chilled. Offer it as a first course or as a light meal when accompanied by hot Tandoori Bread (see page 192).

14 oz.	zucchini, coarsely chopped
1-inch	cube of fresh ginger, peeled and coarsely chopped
1	small green chili, seeded and chopped
1 oz.	desiccated coconut
2 tablespoons	chopped cilantro
1 teaspoon	salt or to taste
1 teaspoon	sugar
¼ teaspoon	freshly ground black pepper
1 tablespoon	lime juice
5½ oz.	low-fat natural yogurt
2½ fl. oz.	fat-free half-and-half

✦ Put the zucchini, ginger, chili, and coconut in a saucepan and add 15 fl. oz. water. Bring to a boil, cover the pan, and reduce the heat to low. Cook for 8–10 minutes.

✦ Remove the pan from the heat and allow the soup to cool for 5–6 minutes, then purée it in a blender until smooth, adding the remaining ingredients except the half-and-half.

✦ Return the soup to the rinsed-out saucepan, add the half-and-half, and heat gently for 2–3 minutes without boiling.

✦ Serve immediately or chill before serving.

Fish Tikka
Machchi Tikka

Servings: 4
Preparation time: 10–15 minutes, plus marinating
Cooking time: 10 minutes
Per serving: Calories: 415; Fat: 27 g.; Saturated fat: 8 g.

Delicate salmon may seem an unlikely match for Indian spices, but a carefully chosen, subtle blend of spices enhances the wonderful natural flavor of the fish.

pinch	saffron threads, pounded
1 tablespoon	hot milk
4½ oz.	modified low-fat plain yogurt (see page 10)
2½ oz.	low-fat sour cream
1½ tablespoons	Ginger Purée (see page 17)
1 tablespoon	Garlic Purée (see page 16)
1½ teaspoons	salt or to taste
½ teaspoon	sugar
½ tablespoons	lemon juice
½ teaspoon	ground turmeric
½ teaspoon	chili powder
½ teaspoon	Garam Masala (see page 23)
1 teaspoon	ground aniseed
1½ lb.	fresh salmon fillets, skinned and cut into 2-inch cubes

Serve with . . .

mild salad onion slices, cucumber slices, and crisp lettuce leaves.

- Soak the pounded saffron in the hot milk for 10 minutes.
- Put the remaining ingredients, except the fish, in a large bowl. Beat until smooth.

→ Stir in the saffron and milk until well mixed, then add the fish. Stir gently until the marinade coats the fish fully. Cover the bowl and set aside in a cool place for 2–3 hours.

→ Preheat the grill on high for 10 minutes. Remove the grid from the grill pan and line the pan with aluminum foil. Lightly brush the foil with oil. Brush 4 metal skewers lightly with oil.

→ Thread the fish on to the prepared skewers, leaving a slight gap between each piece. Place the skewers on the prepared grill pan and grill them about 3 inches away from the heat source for 4–5 minutes.

→ Turn the skewers over and spread any remaining marinade over the fish. Cook for an additional 4–5 minutes or until the fish is slightly charred. Turn the skewers over two or three times during the last 2 minutes of the cooking time.

→ Meanwhile, arrange the mild salad onions, cucumber, and lettuce on plates. Place the skewers on the plates and serve immediately.

Tandoori Chicken
TANDOORI MURGH

SERVINGS: 4
PREPARATION TIME: 20–25 minutes, plus marinating
COOKING TIME: 20 minutes
PER SERVING: Calories: 174; Fat: 5 g.; Saturated fat: 1 g.

One of the most popular Indian dishes, tandoori chicken is relatively easy to cook without fat and it is delicious. I prefer tandoori chicken to have the rich golden color of turmeric with charred patches on the surface, but if you want to add food coloring, you can buy it in powdered form from Indian stores. Chaat masala (available from Indian or Pakistani stores) is a spice mix that is sprinkled on hot tandoori chicken. Athough this is optional, it is worth trying as it transforms the flavor dramatically.

4	chicken breasts or thighs, skinned
	juice of ½ lemon
½ teaspoon	salt
2½ oz.	modified low-fat plain yogurt (see page 10)
1	small onion, coarsely chopped
1 tablespoon	Garlic Purée (see page 16)
1 tablespoon	Ginger Purée (see page 17)
½–1 teaspoon	chili powder
2 teaspoons	ground coriander
1 teaspoon	ground cumin
½ teaspoon	Garam Masala (see page 23)
½ teaspoon	ground turmeric
1 teaspoon	chaat masala (optional)

Garnish with . . .
crisp lettuce leaves, cucumber slices, tomatoes slices, onion rings, or lemon wedges.

➤ Score the chicken pieces all over with a sharp knife, then rub in the lemon juice and salt. Set aside for 15–20 minutes.

➤ Purée the remaining ingredients, except the chaat masala, in a blender until smooth. Pour the mixture over the chicken and rub in well. Leave to marinate in a covered container for 4–6 hours or overnight in the refrigerator. Bring to room temperature before cooking.

➤ Preheat the grill to high. Line the grill pan (without the rack) with aluminum foil. Place the chicken on the foil, reserving the marinade left in the container. Cook about 5 inches below the heat source for 4–5 minutes. Turn the chicken and cook for an additional 4–5 minutes.

➤ Baste the chicken generously with the reserved marinade and cook nearer the heat source, about 4 inches away, for 5–6 minutes or until charred in patches. Turn the chicken and baste with the remaining marinade. Continue to cook for an additional 5–6 minutes or until charred in patches.

➤ Meanwhile, arrange the garnishing ingredients on a serving dish. Transfer the chicken to the dish and sprinkle with the chaat masala. Serve immediately.

COOK'S TIP: For young children, omit the chili powder when preparing the marinade, then add it to the marinade before basting and brush it over the portions to be served to adults.

Chicken Tikka
Murgh Tikka

SERVINGS: 4–5
PREPARATION TIME: 20 minutes, plus marinating
COOKING TIME: 12–13 minutes
PER SERVING: Calories: 360; Fat: 15.5 g.; Saturated fat: 6 g.

Chicken tikka is usually basted with butter or oil during cooking, but a fat-free basting sauce is used in this recipe to keep the chicken moist and succulent.

2 lbs.	chicken breast fillets, skinned and cut into 2-inch cubes
1 tablespoon	lemon juice
1¼ teaspoons	salt or to taste
pinch	saffron threads, pounded
1 tablespoon	hot milk
1 teaspoon	sugar
4½ oz.	modified low-fat plain yogurt (see page 10)
4½ fl. oz.	fat-free half-and-half
1 tablespoon	Garlic Purée (see page 16)
1 tablespoon	Ginger Purée (see page 17)
½ teaspoon	ground turmeric
1 teaspoon	Garam Masala (see page 23)
½ teaspoon	chili powder
½ teaspoon	Ground Roasted Coriander (see page 22)
½ teaspoon	Ground Roasted Cumin (see page 21)
2 teaspoons	besan (gram or chickpea flour)
1 tablespoon	very finely chopped fresh cilantro leaves

Serve with . . .
a green salad.

➤ Put the chicken in a bowl and rub the lemon juice and salt well into the pieces. Set aside for 30 minutes.

→ Meanwhile, soak the saffron in the milk for 20 minutes.

→ Mix the sugar, yogurt, fat-free half-and-half, garlic and ginger purées, turmeric, and garam masala. Add to the chicken to coat. Cover and marinate for 3 hours in the refrigerator. Bring to room temperature before cooking.

→ Preheat the grill to high and line a grill pan (without the rack) with aluminum foil. Lightly brush the foil and 5–6 metal skewers with oil.

→ Thread the chicken onto the skewers, reserving the marinade, and place in the grill pan. Grill 3 inches away from the heat for 5 minutes.

→ Meanwhile, mix the remaining ingredients with the reserved marinade and brush the chicken with this mixture. Cook for 3–4 minutes.

→ Turn the chicken and baste with the remaining marinade. Cook for 2–3 minutes, or until slightly charred.

Silky Chicken Kebabs

Reshmi Kabab

SERVINGS: 18
PREPARATION TIME: 10 minutes, plus chilling
COOKING TIME: 8–10 minutes
PER SERVING: Calories: 50; Fat: 2.5 g.; Saturated fat: 0.6 g.

The word *resham* means silk and the soft, smooth texture of these kebabs is their main characteristic. They're great with drinks and, if made slightly bigger, they can also be served as a starter, with a relish or salad. Wrapped in chapatis or bought wheat tortillas, and served with a relish, they can make a filling meal.

2 oz.	unroasted cashew nut pieces
1	egg
1 lb.	ground chicken
2 teaspoons	Garlic Purée (see page 16)
2 teaspoons	Ginger Purée (see page 17)
1–3	green chilies, seeded and chopped
½ oz.	fresh cilantro leaves and stalks
2 teaspoons	Ground Roasted Coriander (see page 22)
1 teaspoon	Garam Masala (see page 23)
1 teaspoon	salt or to taste

Basting Sauce

1 tablespoon	low-fat plain yogurt
½ teaspoon	paprika
¼–½ teaspoon	chili powder
½ teaspoon	dried mint

➔ Blend the cashews and egg in a food processor for a few seconds.
➔ Add the remaining ingredients (except for the basting sauce) and blend until smooth. Transfer the mixture to a bowl, cover and chill for 30 minutes.

- Preheat the grill to high for 10 minutes. Line a grill pan (without the rack) with aluminum foil and brush it lightly with oil.
- Have a bowl of water ready to wet your fingers before you start shaping the kebabs. This will stop the mixture from sticking to your fingers. Wet your fingers and divide the mixture in half, then make 9 portions out of each half.
- Shape each portion into a sausage shape, about 3 inches long, and place in the prepared grill pan. Dip your fingers in the water occasionally to prevent the mixture from sticking to them.
- Grill the kebabs 3 inches below the heat source for 3 minutes. Turn them over and cook for an additional 3 minutes.
- Meanwhile, make the basting sauce. Blend the yogurt with 1 tablespoon water until smooth, then mix in all the remaining ingredients and brush generously over the kebabs.
- Cook the kebabs for 1 minute, then turn them over, brush with the remaining basting sauce, and cook for an additional 1 minute. Serve hot or cold.

COOK'S TIP: If cooking for children as well as adults, omit the chilies and set a portion of the kebab mixture aside, then add the chilies and blend again to make the spicier kebabs.

Ground Lamb Kebabs

SHAMI KABAB

SERVINGS: 4
PREPARATION TIME: 15–20 minutes, plus chilling
COOKING TIME: 12–14 minutes
PER SERVING: Calories: 52; Fat: 2.3 g.; Saturated fat: 1 g.

The Indian kabab is said to be a nomadic invention, suited to a roving lifestyle, and brought to India by the Middle Eastern invaders who knew the dish as kebab. Normally, these kebabs are fried, but in this recipe, the ingredients have been adjusted for grilling without added fat and without sacrificing flavor.

2½ oz.	channa dhal (see page 12)
1–3	dried red chilies
4½ oz.	low-fat plain yogurt
1	large egg
2-inch cube	fresh ginger, peeled and coarsely chopped
3–4	garlic cloves, coarsely chopped
2–3 tablespoons	chopped fresh cilantro leaves
12–15	fresh mint leaves
1–2	green chilies, seeded and chopped
1½ teaspoons	Ground Roasted Coriander (see page 22)
1 teaspoon	Garam Masala (see page 23)
1 teaspoon	salt
1	small onion, coarsely chopped
1 tablespoon	lemon juice
1 lb., 2 oz.	lean ground lamb

→ Wash the channa dhal and soak for 2–3 hours.
→ Drain the dhal and put in a saucepan with the red chilies. Add 6 fl. oz. water, bring to a boil and reduce the heat to medium-low. Cook, uncovered, for 7–8 minutes or until the liquid has evaporated.

→ Put the cooked dhal in a food processor and add the yogurt and egg. Blend until the dhal is fine, then add the remaining ingredients. Blend until smooth. Chill the mixture for 1 hour or overnight in an airtight container.

→ Preheat the grill to high for 8–10 minutes and line a grill pan (without the rack) with aluminum foil. Brush the foil lightly with oil.

→ Have a bowl of water ready before you start shaping the kebabs. Dip your fingers in the water occasionally as you shape 24 golf-ball-sized portions. Flatten each ball by rotating between your palms, then pressing down gently.

→ Place the kebabs in the prepared grill pan and cook them 3 inches below the heat source for 3–4 minutes on each side. Serve immediately.

COOK'S TIP: You can serve these kebabs in pita bread with a relish of your choice to make a main meal. If you make them bigger than in the above recipe, they can be served with salad as a starter.

Indian Cheese Kebabs

PANEER KA KABAB

SERVINGS: 4–5
PREPARATION TIME: 20 minutes, plus marinating
COOKING TIME: 10 minutes
PER SERVING: Calories: 136; Fat: 4 g.; Saturated fat: 1 g.

Here is an attractive and delicious vegetarian tandoori dish that you can cook under a hot grill. Paneer is full of essential nutrients and has as much protein as meat and poultry—a great source of protein for vegetarians. It is available in large supermarkets and Indian stores. You could use tofu instead, or Cypriot halloumi cheese, but do not use salt with halloumi because, unlike paneer and tofu, it is already salted. You can use either metal or bamboo skewers. If using bamboo, soak them in cold water for 30 minutes to stop them burning under the grill.

7 oz.	paneer, cut into 1-inch cubes (see page 11)
8 oz.	potatoes, boiled in their skins until tender but still firm, peeled and cut into 1-inch cubes
8	shallots, halved
4½ oz.	red pepper, seeded and cut into 1-inch cubes
4½ oz.	button mushrooms, halved
1 tablespoon	sunflower or canola oil
1 teaspoon	Ground Roasted Cumin (see page 21)

Marinade

2 tablespoons	lemon juice
2 teaspoons	Ginger Purée (see page 17)
2 teaspoons	Garlic Purée (see page 16)
2 teaspoons	ground coriander
½–1 teaspoon	chili powder
½ teaspoon	ground turmeric

1 teaspoon	salt or to taste
3 oz.	low-fat plain yogurt
2 teaspoons	besan (gram or chickpea flour), blended to a paste with 2 tablespoons water

Garnish with . . .

finely shredded crisp lettuce leaves and cherry tomatoes.

→ Bring a pan full of water to a boil and add the cubes of paneer. Bring back to a boil and cook for 1 minute. Drain and allow to cool (this enables the cheese to absorb the spices).

→ In a large bowl, mix together all the ingredients for the marinade.

→ Add the paneer, potatoes, shallots, red pepper, and mushrooms and mix thoroughly. Cover with plastic wrap and refrigerate for 3–4 hours. You can leave overnight, but bring it to room temperature before cooking.

→ Preheat the grill on high for 5–6 minutes. Remove the grid from the grill pan and line the pan with aluminum foil. Lightly brush the foil with oil.

→ Brush 4–5 skewers lightly with oil and thread the marinated paneer and vegetables on to them. Make sure you shake off any excess marinade back into the bowl and alternate the ingredients evenly on the skewers. Place the skewers on the prepared grill pan and grill them about 3 inches away from the heat source for 2–3 minutes.

→ Add 1 tablespoon water to the marinade left in the bowl and mix it well with the remaining oil. Brush some of the marinade over the kebabs and cook for an additional 2–3 minutes. Turn the skewers over and brush with the remaining marinade. Continue to cook for 3–4 minutes or until the kebabs are browned.

→ Remove from the heat and sprinkle the cumin evenly over all the skewers. Serve garnished with lettuce leaves and cherry tomatoes.

COOK'S TIP: Besides serving these kebabs as starters, you can make a substantial vegetarian meal by serving them with a lentil dish, and rice or bread.

Pork Kebabs

SHIKAR KA KABAB

SERVINGS: 16
PREPARATION TIME: 15 minutes
COOKING TIME: 20 minutes
PER SERVING: Calories: 43; Fat: 2 g.; Saturated fat: 0.7 g.

This recipe is based on the idea of wrapping kebabs in leaves and cooking them in a tandoor (clay oven). Banana leaves are traditional, but they have to be thrown away when they have imparted their distinctive flavor to the kebabs. I prefer cabbage leaves because you can eat them, particularly in this recipe, where the kebabs are steamed. The delicious juicy cabbage leaves taste excellent with the superb, subtle flavors of the meat inside.

16	large green cabbage leaves
1 lb.	lean ground pork
1 tablespoon	grated fresh ginger
1 teaspoon	Garlic Purée (see page 16)
1–2	green chilies, seeded and chopped
1 tablespoon	finely chopped cilantro
2 tablespoons	finely chopped red onion
½ teaspoon	Garam Masala (see page 23)
1 teaspoon	salt or to taste

➜ Blanch the cabbage leaves in boiling salted water for 5 minutes. Drain and refresh in cold water. Leave to drain in a colander, then pat dry with a paper towel. Carefully remove the central stem from each leaf without tearing or cutting through the rest of the leaf.

➜ Combine the meat with the remaining ingredients and knead until smooth. Divide the mixture into 16 equal portions and shape each into a flat cake.

➜ Place a portion of meat on a cabbage leaf and fold the leaf around it to make a neat parcel. Tie the parcel with kitchen string. Repeat with the remaining leaves and portions of meat.

➜ Prepare a steamer over a saucepan of boiling water. Place the parcels in the steamer and cook for 20 minutes. Serve with Fresh Tomato Chutney (see page 227).

Variation:

Use ground chicken or turkey instead of the pork.

Steamed Pork Balls

SHIKAR KOFTAS

SERVINGS: 6–8
PREPARATION TIME: 25 minutes
COOKING TIME: 20 minutes
PER SERVING: Calories: 114; Fat: 5 g.; Saturated fat: 1.8 g.

This is a traditional Tibetan recipe with extraordinary flavors. To fit into the low fat principle of the book, I have omitted the pastry that the Tibetans use to wrap the spiced pork before steaming. Serve the little meatballs with Fresh Tomato Chutney (see page 227) at cocktail parties: They'll be a big hit.

1 lb.	lean ground pork
2-inch	cube of fresh ginger, peeled and coarsely chopped
1–2	green chilies, seeded and coarsely chopped
1 teaspoon	salt or to taste
1	large egg
4	scallions, white part only, finely chopped

+ Put the pork in a food processor and switch on the machine for a few seconds.
+ Add the remaining ingredients, except the scallions, and process until you have a smooth paste.
+ Transfer the mixture to a large bowl and add the scallions. Mix well.
+ Have a bowl of water ready. Dip the fingers of both your hands in the water (this will prevent the meat paste from sticking to your fingers) and make small balls, which should be slightly smaller than walnuts. You should be able to make 25–27 meatballs.
+ Prepare a steamer over a saucepan of boiling water. Put the meatballs in the steamer and cook for 20 minutes. If you do not have a steamer, put a rack in a saucepan and pour in water to come slightly below the rack. Bring just to a boil. Put the meatballs on a plate and place on the rack. Cover the pan and steam for 20 minutes. Check that the water doesn't evaporate completely and add boiling water if necessary.
+ Serve hot or cold (not chilled).

Cottage Cheese Canapés
PANEER PURI

SERVINGS: 8–10
PREPARATION TIME: 10–15 minutes
PER SERVING: Calories: 25; Fat: 0.4 g.; Saturated fat: 0.2 g.

*I*ndian cottage cheese is known as paneer, but I have used low-fat Western cottage cheese for this recipe. Traditionally served on puri—deep-fried crispy bread—I have used water crackers and sliced cucumber instead.

8 oz.	low-fat cottage cheese
1/2	red onion, finely chopped
1/4 teaspoon	salt or to taste
1/4–1/2 teaspoon	chili powder
1/4 teaspoon	Ground Roasted Cumin (see page 21)
1 tablespoon	finely chopped fresh cilantro leaves

Serve with . . .
   cucumber slices, and/or small crackers.

Garnish with . . .
   paprika or chili powder, Ground Roasted Cumin (see page 21).

→ Mix the cottage cheese with the remaining ingredients.
→ Carefully spoon the cheese mixture onto cucumber slices and small water crackers just before serving. Sprinkle with a little paprika or chili and cumin, and serve immediately.

Spiced Potato Canapés

PAPRI CHAAT

SERVINGS: 8–10
PREPARATION TIME: 20 minutes
COOKING TIME: 15–20 minutes
PER SERVING: Calories: 80; Fat: 2 g.; Saturated fat: 0.09 g.

One of the most popular snacks in north India is deep-fried crispy bread topped with potatoes and tamarind sauce. The word *chaat* means "finger-licking good" and even though this is a fat-free version, it is lip-smacking good too!

8 oz.	potatoes, boiled in their skins and cooled
4½ oz.	low-fat plain yogurt
½ teaspoon	chili powder
1	small green chili, seeded and finely chopped
1 tablespoon	finely chopped fresh cilantro leaves
1–2 tablespoons	finely chopped red onion
½ teaspoon	salt or to taste
1	packet small water crackers
1	quantity Date and Raisin Chutney (see page 226)

→ Peel the potatoes and chop them very finely. Put them into a mixing bowl.

→ Mix the yogurt with the chili powder, green chili, cilantro, onion, and salt. Pour the mixture over the potatoes and mix thoroughly.

→ Pile about 2 teaspoons potato mixture on each cracker and top with chutney to taste—try a heaped teaspoon first, then adjust the quantity to your liking.

COOK'S TIP: You can make an instant relish to top the potatoes by mixing 1½ tablespoons tamarind juice with ¼ teaspoon each of chili powder and salt, and ½ teaspoon each of sugar and Ground Roasted Cumin (see page 21).

Spiced Corn-on-the-Cob
MASALEDAR BHUTTA

SERVINGS: 4
PREPARATION TIME: 10 minutes
COOKING TIME: 25–30 minutes
PER SERVING: Calories: 132; Fat: 2.8 g.; Saturated fat: 0.4 g.

Corn is grown extensively in the state of Punjab, where it is used for various delicacies, including corn bread (*makki ki roti*), the staple on which the people thrive. Here, the cobs of corn are steamed, then brushed with a light seasoning of spice to make a delicious snack or starter. They can also be cooked on the barbecue; whichever cooking method is used, always wrap the corn in aluminum foil to prevent the cobs from drying out.

4	large cobs of corn
	juice of 1 lime
½ teaspoon	salt
½ teaspoon	Ground Roasted Cumin (see page 21)
½ teaspoon	chili powder or to taste
¼ teaspoon	dried mint

❖ Prepare a steamer over a saucepan of boiling water. Wrap the corn individually in aluminum foil and place in the steamer. Cook for 25–30 minutes.

❖ Meanwhile, mix the lime juice with the remaining ingredients. Brush the spice mixture over the corn and serve immediately.

Fish Salad
MACHCHI SALAT

SERVINGS: 6–8
PREPARATION TIME: 10–15 minutes, plus chilling
PER SERVING: Calories: 150; Fat: 13 g.; Saturated fat: 2.6 g.

*M*y grandmother used to smoke fish to make this salad, which she served with boiled basmati rice and Lentils with Hot Oil Seasoning (see page 168). Whenever I make this salad, I can almost smell the aromas that wafted from my grandmother's kitchen.

9 oz.	smoked mackerel, skinned
2 tablespoons	finely chopped red onions
1	green chili, seeded and finely chopped
2 tablespoons	finely chopped cilantro
2 tablespoons	lime juice

Serve with . . .
an assortment of raw ingredients, such as cucumber slices, short lengths of celery sticks, and cherry tomatoes (seeded and with pulp removed). This dish is also delicious with crackers.

- ➜ Coarsely mash the fish with a fork.
- ➜ Add the remaining ingredients and chill for 30 minutes.
- ➜ Pile small mounds of the mixture on cucumber slices or into celery sticks or cherry tomatoes.

Serve with . . .
a small portion of any bread for a first course. Alternatively, you can serve this dish on crackers with drinks.

 COOK'S TIP: The mixture also makes a delicious sandwich filling. For young children, remove a portion of the salad before adding the chili.

Stuffed Peppers

BHARWAN SIMLA MIRCHI

SERVINGS: 4
PREPARATION TIME: 15–20 minutes
COOKING TIME: 20–25 minutes
PER SERVING: Calories: 196; Fat: 7 g.; Saturated fat: 0.8 g.

With its striking appearance, this simple and nutritious vegetarian starter cannot fail to tempt. The peppers can also make a main meal for two if served with a salad and Puffed Grilled Bread (see page 194) or Spiced Chapatis (see page 190).

2	green or red peppers
1½ tablespoons	sunflower or canola oil
½ teaspoon	black mustard seeds
½ teaspoon	cumin seeds
1	small red onion, finely chopped
1	green or red chili, seeded and chopped
¼ teaspoon	ground turmeric
½ teaspoon	chili powder (optional)
1 teaspoon	Ground Roasted Coriander (see page 22)
14 oz.	canned chickpeas, drained and rinsed
¼–½ teaspoon	salt
2 tablespoons	finely chopped fresh cilantro leaves
1 tablespoon	lime juice
1 tablespoon	whole wheat flour

Serve with . . .
cucumber slices and lettuce leaves.

➤ Carefully halve the peppers lengthwise, keeping the pieces of stalk intact in both halves. Remove the seeds and the pith and brush the skin lightly with oil. Set aside.
➤ Preheat the oven to 375°F. Line a roasting tin with foil.

→ Heat the remaining oil in a nonstick saucepan over low heat and add the mustard seeds. When they crackle, add the cumin seeds then the onion and chili. Increase the heat and fry for 3–4 minutes, stirring.

→ Reduce the heat to low and add the turmeric, chili powder (if using), and ground coriander. Cook for 30 seconds, then add the chickpeas. Cook for 1 minute and add the salt, cilantro, and lime juice. Stir to mix well.

→ Pour in 2½ fl. oz. water and add the flour. Stir until the water has been absorbed. Remove from the heat and divide the mixture among the pepper halves. Place on the prepared roasting tin.

→ Cook for 15 minutes.

Fish Dishes

INDIA HAS A vast coastline and the entire land is latticed with rivers and lakes, so it isn't surprising that the country has a thriving industry specializing in exporting some of the finest-quality seafood. Indian cooks take full advantage of the abundant supply of fish to create an extensive repertoire of recipes, but I am always saddened by the lack of fish and seafood dishes on menus in Indian restaurants.

Buying and storing fish properly are just as important as cooking it successfully. Always make sure that the fish is absolutely fresh: the most obvious sign of freshness is the eyes, which should be shiny and full. Fish should look moist and glistening, and feel firm to the touch. Never leave fish at room temperature, even for a short time, but store it promptly in the refrigerator. Cook fish as soon as possible after purchase, ideally on the same day.

Fish is a highly nutritious protein food, and white fish is low in fat. Oily fish, such as salmon and mackerel, contain fats that contribute to healthy eating. Recent research indicates that the omega-3 fatty acids found in oily fish offer protection against coronary diseases.

Arunachal Fish Curry
Pa Chao

SERVINGS: 4
PREPARATION TIME: 15–20 minutes, plus standing
COOKING TIME: 10 minutes
PER SERVING: Calories: 315; Fat: 20 g.; Saturated fat: 6 g.

When I was in India recently, my friend Fantry Jaswal cooked this fish curry for me. Fantry comes from the beautiful district of Arunachal Pradesh in the Himalayan foothills and it is from her that I learned to appreciate the flavors of tribal food. I modified the recipe slightly, but it retains the original characteristics. You can also use any firm white fish instead of salmon.

4	salmon steaks, halved
1 teaspoon	salt or to taste
1 tablespoon	lemon juice
¼–½ teaspoon	chili powder
½ teaspoon	ground turmeric
6 oz.	canned chopped tomatoes with their juice or fresh tomatoes, skinned and chopped
½ oz.	fresh cilantro leaves and stalks
1–2	green chilies, seeded and chopped
1	large garlic clove, coarsely chopped
1-inch	cubes of fresh ginger, peeled and coarsely chopped
1 oz.	desiccated coconut

→ Lay the pieces of fish on a large plate and sprinkle with half the salt, the lemon juice, chili powder and turmeric. Rub gently with your fingertips and set aside for 15–20 minutes.

→ Purée the remaining ingredients, except the coconut, in a blender. Grind the coconut in a spice or coffee mill until smooth.

→ Put the puréed ingredients in a nonstick saucepan, about 12 inches in diameter, and add the coconut and remaining salt. Heat over low heat, stirring, until heated through.

✦ Add the fish to the pan in a single layer on the sauce. Cover and cook for 7–8 minutes. Shake the pan from side to side 2 or 3 times and spoon some of the hot sauce over the fish.

✦ Remove from the heat and serve with boiled basmati rice and Cabbage with Ginger (see page 206).

COOK'S TIP: It is important to grind the coconut so that you have a smooth sauce. If you do not have a coffee mill, soak the coconut in boiling water (just enough to cover it), then drain it and add to the ingredients in the blender. It will take longer to achieve a smooth texture in the blender.

Fish with Lentil Sauce

DHAN-DHAL-PATIO

SERVINGS: 4
PREPARATION TIME: 15–20 minutes
COOKING TIME: 30–35 minutes
PER SERVING: Calories: 240; Fat: 6.6 g.; Saturated fat: .85 g.

This is one of the superb contributions made to Indian cuisine by a small community known as the Parsees, who came to India about thirteen centuries ago from their Persian homeland. A little oil is necessary here to achieve the authentic flavor. Served with boiled basmati rice, this makes a complete meal, especially when accompanied by a salad or raita for a healthy balance.

2 tablespoons	sunflower or canola oil
½ teaspoon	cumin seeds
2 teaspoons	Garlic Purée (see page 16)
2 teaspoons	Ginger Purée (see page 17)
4½ oz.	red lentils, washed and drained
½ teaspoon	ground turmeric
1	green chili, seeded and chopped
13½ fl. oz.	warm water
1 teaspoon	salt or to taste
½	onion, finely chopped
4½ oz.	tomatoes, skinned and chopped
½ teaspoon	Ground Roasted Cumin (see page 21)
½ teaspoon	Ground Roasted Coriander (see page 22)
½ teaspoon	chili powder
¼ teaspoon	Garam Masala (see page 23)
¼ teaspoon	tamarind concentrate (or 1 tablespoon tamarind juice)
½ teaspoon	sugar
14 oz.	peeled raw king prawns
2 tablespoons	finely chopped fresh cilantro

Serve with . . .

boiled basmati rice.

→ Heat half the oil in a nonstick pan over low heat. Add the cumin seeds, followed by half the garlic and ginger purées. Fry for 1 minute.

→ Add the lentils, half the turmeric and the chili. Increase the heat slightly and fry for 2–3 minutes, stirring constantly.

→ Pour in 11½ fl. oz. of the water and bring to a boil. Reduce the heat to low, cover the pan and cook for 25–30 minutes. Add a little more water (in addition to the total quantity in the ingredients list) if necessary; the dhal should resemble a thick batter when cooked. Stir in half the salt and remove from the heat.

→ While the lentils are cooking, heat the remaining oil in a nonstick saucepan over medium heat. Add the onion and the remaining garlic and ginger purées. Fry for 2 minutes, then reduce the heat slightly and continue to fry for an additional 1–2 minutes.

→ Stir in the tomatoes, cumin, ground coriander, chili powder, garam masala, and the remaining turmeric. Cook for 2 minutes, then add the remaining 1¾ fl. oz. water. Continue to cook for 2–3 minutes, stirring frequently.

→ Stir in the remaining salt, the tamarind and sugar. If using tamarind concentrate, stir until it has dissolved.

→ Add the prawns, increase the heat slightly and cook for 5–7 minutes, stirring frequently. Sprinkle in a little water if necessary. Add the cilantro and remove from the heat.

→ Serve a portion of dhal on boiled basmati rice and top with the prawns.

COOK'S TIP: You can use any firm white fish or prawns. I have used raw king prawns, but cooked small or king prawns can be used—simply toss them gently in the spices until heated through. If you cannot get either tamarind concentrate or juice, use 1 tablespoon lime juice.

Baked Fish
Dum Machchi

SERVINGS: 4
PREPARATION TIME: 10 minutes
COOKING TIME: 1 hour
PER SERVING: Calories: 215; Fat: 5 g.; Saturated fat: 1.5 g.

This makes an easy and tasty mid-week meal. It takes only a few minutes to combine the ingredients, then the dish is simply placed in the oven and you are free to relax.

1¼ lbs.	cod or haddock fillet, skinned and cut in chunks
8 oz.	potatoes, boiled and coarsely chopped
1-inch	cube of fresh ginger, coarsely chopped
2	large garlic cloves, coarsely chopped
1–2	green chilies, seeded and chopped
½ oz.	fresh cilantro leaves and stalks
1 teaspoon	salt or to taste
½ teaspoon	ground aniseed
½ teaspoon	ground turmeric
2	large eggs
5 fl. oz.	2% milk
2 teaspoons	chopped fresh dill
¼	red pepper, seeded and finely chopped

➜ Preheat the oven to 375°F.
➜ Blend all the ingredients, except the dill and red pepper, in a food processor until smooth.
➜ Lightly brush a 9-inch nonstick ring mold with oil and sprinkle the base of the ring with the dill and red pepper.
➜ Pack the fish mixture into the ring and bake for 1 hour or until the top is lightly browned.
➜ Use a knife to loosen the edge of the fish mixture around the rim of the mold. Cover

the top of the mold with a serving platter, then invert both platter and mold. Lift off the mold. Serve immediately, with Kohlrabi Salad (see page 232) and any bread.

COOK'S TIP: The mixture can be puréed in a blender, but you will have to do it in batches, then mix them all together in a bowl.

Dry-Spiced Grilled Fish
Sukha Masaledar Machchi

SERVINGS: 4
PREPARATION TIME: 10 minutes, plus marinating
COOKING TIME: 7–8 minutes
PER SERVING: Calories: 296; Fat: 19 g.; Saturated fat: 3 g.

*I*f you are a fish lover, you will find this delicately spiced dish to be divine. Succulent chunks of salmon perfumed with coriander and a touch of chili and garlic will leave you craving for more! You do need oily fish for this—my second choice is rainbow trout when salmon steaks aren't available.

2 tablespoons	lemon juice
1 teaspoon	Garlic Purée (see page 16)
1 teaspoon	Ginger Purée (see page 17)
¼–½ teaspoon	chili powder
½ teaspoon	salt
4	salmon steaks
1 tablespoon	sunflower or canola oil
1½ teaspoons	Ground Roasted Coriander (see page 22)
1 tablespoon	very finely chopped fresh cilantro leaves

→ Mix the lemon juice, garlic and ginger purées, chili powder, and salt.

→ Lay the salmon steaks on a large plate or dish and gently rub the seasoning mixture into them. Cover and set aside to marinate for 30 minutes.

→ Preheat the grill to high and line a grill pan (without the rack) with aluminum foil. Brush the foil lightly with oil and arrange the prepared fish on the foil.

→ Cook the fish about 5 inches away from the heat source for 3–4 minutes.

→ Meanwhile, mix the oil, ground coriander, and fresh cilantro together. Turn the fish over, taking care not to break the steaks. Divide the coriander mixture equally among the steaks, spreading it gently to cover them completely.

→ Grill the salmon for an additional 2–3 minutes, then serve immediately. The salmon steaks are delicious served with Savory Potato Mash (see page 197) and Almond Chutney (see page 225) or a lentil dish and Cinnamon Rice (see page 175).

Jumbo Shrimp with Baby Zucchini

JHINGA AUR GHIA

SERVINGS: 2–4
PREPARATION TIME: 10 minutes
COOKING TIME: 10 minutes
PER SERVING: Calories: 240; Fat: 15 g.; Saturated fat: 12 g.

*S*ucculent shrimp and baby zucchini look striking together. The characteristic taste here comes from freshly grated ginger root and curry leaves, which have the most captivating flavor combined with an enticing aroma. This quantity will serve two people as a main meal with Cumin-Coriander Rice (see page 174) or boiled basmati rice. Served with rice plus a lentil and a vegetable dish, it will easily feed four.

If you are generally following a low-fat diet, you can certainly indulge yourself occasionally. As this recipe has a higher fat content, perhaps you could treat yourself on a Sunday or cook it for a special dinner party.

8 oz.	baby zucchini
3 fl. oz.	reduced-fat coconut milk
3 fl. oz.	water
½ teaspoon	ground aniseed
1 teaspoon	grated fresh ginger
½ teaspoon	salt or to taste
½ teaspoon	crushed dried red chilies
12–16	fresh or dried curry leaves
8 oz.	jumbo shrimp, peeled and cooked
1 tablespoon	lime juice
1 tablespoon	finely chopped fresh cilantro leaves

→ Slit the zucchini lengthwise in half and set aside.

→ Put the coconut milk, water, ground aniseed, ginger, salt, and crushed chilies together in a bowl and mix well.

→ Put the zucchini in a wide shallow pan and add the coconut milk mixture and the curry leaves. Place over medium-low heat, bring to a slow simmer and cook, uncovered, for 5 minutes.

→ Add the shrimp, cover, and cook for 5 minutes. Stir in the lime juice and fresh coriander and remove from the heat. Serve immediately.

Fish Cakes
Machchi Tikki

SERVINGS: 12
PREPARATION TIME: 20–25 minutes, plus chilling
COOKING TIME: 12–15 minutes
PER SERVING: Calories: 80; Fat: 2.3 g.; Saturated fat: 0.4 g.

*Y*ou will need a heavy nonstick frying pan because only a little oil is brushed lightly over it and the fish cakes are cooked until browned. Make half the quantity if you wish to serve them as a starter; shaped into cocktail-size cakes, they're also a delicious dish to serve with drinks.

2	thick slices of white bread, 1–2 days old, crusts removed and cut into cubes
1	large egg
1-inch	cube of fresh ginger, peeled and chopped
2	large garlic cloves, chopped
3 tablespoons	coarsely chopped fresh cilantro leaves and stalks
1–2	green chilies, seeded and chopped
1¼ lbs.	white fish fillet, skinned
4½ oz.	potatoes, boiled and coarsely chopped
½ teaspoon	ground aniseed
¼ teaspoon	ground turmeric
1 teaspoon	salt or to taste
1	small onion, coarsely chopped
1½ tablespoons	sunflower or canola oil

→ Put the bread in a food processor and add the egg, ginger, garlic, fresh coriander, and chilies. Process until smooth.

→ Add the remaining ingredients, except the oil, and blend by pulsing the power on and off until the mixture has a slightly coarse texture. Transfer the mixture to a suitable container, cover and chill for 30 minutes.

→ Divide the mixture in half and shape 6 equal-sized cakes, about $\frac{1}{4}$-inch thick, from each half.

→ Heat a heavy nonstick frying pan over medium heat and brush a little oil over the entire surface. Heat again for 1–2 minutes, then cook the fish cakes in batches, adding a little extra oil as necessary and spreading it with a brush each time. Allow 2–3 minutes on each side or until the fish cakes are browned.

→ Serve with Spinach Raita (see page 222) or Fresh Tomato Chutney (see page 227) and any bread.

Fish in Coconut Milk

MEEN MOLEE

SERVINGS: 4
PREPARATION TIME: 10–15 minutes
COOKING TIME: 10–12 minutes
PER SERVING: Calories: 340; Fat: 23 g.; Saturated fat: 9 g.

*T*his recipe is adapted from a south Indian recipe in which onions, ginger, chilies, and spices are sautéed in coconut oil before adding coconut milk and fish. To balance this oil-free version, I have also omitted many of the traditional spices and I am delighted with the subtle, but brilliant, flavors. You can use firm-fleshed white fish—such as swordfish, shark, monkfish, or cod—or jumbo shrimp instead of salmon.

4 fl. oz.	reduced-fat coconut milk
4 fl. oz.	water
20	curry leaves, preferably fresh
1/4-inch	cube of fresh ginger, peeled and cut into julienne strips
1 teaspoon	chili powder or to taste
1/2 teaspoon	salt or to taste
4	salmon steaks, halved
2–3	fresh chilies, preferably red
1 tablespoon	chopped fresh cilantro leaves
1 tablespoon	lime juice

➔ Blend the coconut milk with the water in a saucepan, about 12 inches in diameter, with the curry leaves, ginger, chili powder, and salt. Heat until simmering, and simmer for 2–3 minutes.

➔ Add the fish, laying the pieces in the pan in a single layer, and bring slowly back to simmering point. Cover the pan and cook over low heat for 5–6 minutes. Shake the pan from side to side occasionally, but do not stir the curry.

✦ Add the whole chilies, fresh cilantro, and lime juice. Shake the pan as before and simmer for 1–2 minutes. Remove from the heat and serve immediately, with boiled basmati rice and Cabbage Salad (see page 230).

COOK'S TIP: When halving salmon steaks, use a heavy knife (and tap it down with a rolling pin) or poultry shears to cut through the bone. Leaving the bone in helps to keep the fish in shape during cooking.

Fish in Mustard Sauce

Shorshe diya Maach

SERVINGS: 4
PREPARATION TIME: 10–15 minutes, plus marinating
COOKING TIME: 10–12 minutes
PER SERVING: Calories: 145; Fat: 1.3 g.; Saturated fat: 0.18 g.

A specialty from Bengal and Assam, this dish is traditionally cooked in pungent mustard oil with ground mustard. My grandmother always steamed the marinated fish wrapped in banana leaf, which imparted a distinctive flavor. Here, I have omitted the oil and used mustard powder, then wrapped the fish in aluminum foil—the result captures most of the traditional flavors and appearance. Large whole sardines are also excellent prepared in this way.

1½ lbs.	cod, haddock, or halibut fillet, skinned
1½ tablespoons	mustard powder
1½ teaspoons	besan (gram or chickpea flour)
½ teaspoon	ground turmeric
1 teaspoon	salt or to taste
2–3 tablespoons	finely chopped fresh cilantro leaves and stalks
1	red chili, seeded and cut into julienne strips
1	green chili, seeded and cut into julienne strips

→ Cut the fish into 2-inch pieces and place on a large plate.
→ Mix the mustard powder and besan together, then blend to a smooth paste with 2 tablespoons water. If there are any tiny lumps (besan can become lumpy) strain the paste through a fine sieve or strainer.
→ Add the turmeric, salt, and fresh cilantro to the besan paste and mix thoroughly. Spread the paste evenly on the fish, cover, and marinate in the refrigerator for 1–2 hours.

→ When you are ready to cook the fish, prepare a steamer over a saucepan of boiling water.

→ Put half of the fish fillets on a large piece of aluminum foil and arrange half of the chilies on top. Cover with the remaining fish and place the remaining chilies on top. Fold the foil around the fish to enclose it in a neat parcel, folding and pinching the edges to seal them well.

→ Place in the steamer and cook for 10–12 minutes. Serve immediately, with boiled basmati rice and Mixed Vegetable Curry (see page 210).

Fish in Coconut and Coriander Sauce

MASHLI GHASHI

SERVINGS: 4
PREPARATION TIME: 10–15 minutes, plus marinating
COOKING TIME: 12–15 minutes
PER SERVING: Calories: 370; Fat: 26 g.; Saturated fat: 9 g.

This classic dish from the southern coastal region of India is usually prepared with a generous amount of freshly grated coconut, but I have given it an entirely modern taste and reduced the coconut to an acceptable level for a healthy diet. Dill complements salmon so perfectly that I have added it to the sauce, and the transformation in taste and appearance is superb.

4	salmon steaks, halved
1 tablespoon	lemon juice
¼ teaspoon	ground turmeric
1 teaspoon	salt or to taste
1 tablespoon	sunflower or canola oil
1 teaspoon	Ginger Purée (see page 17)
1 teaspoon	Garlic Purée (see page 16)
3¾ fl. oz.	reduced fat coconut milk
3¾ fl. oz.	water
½–1 teaspoon	chili powder
1 teaspoon	Ground Roasted Coriander (see page 22)
1 teaspoon	dried dill

➤ Lay the fish on a flat dish and sprinkle with the lemon juice, turmeric, and half the salt. Gently rub the seasonings into the fish with your finger tips, then set it aside to marinate for 10 minutes.

→ Heat the oil in a nonstick saucepan or frying pan, at least 12 inches in diameter, over low heat. Add the ginger and garlic purées and fry for 1 minute.

→ Pour the coconut milk and water into the pan, followed by the remaining salt, chili powder, and coriander.

→ Lay the salmon steaks in the pan in a single layer. Wait until the sauce begins to bubble gently, then cover the pan and increase the heat slightly. Cook for 3–4 minutes.

→ Remove the lid and cook for an additional 3–4 minutes, then shake the pan from side to side and continue to cook for an additional 2–3 minutes.

→ Sprinkle with the dill, then stir gently to mix and remove from the heat. Serve immediately, with boiled basmati rice and Spiced Green Beans (see page 212).

Leaf-Wrapped Fish
Patra-ni-Machchi

SERVINGS: 4
PREPARATION TIME: 30 minutes
COOKING TIME: 15 minutes
PER SERVING: Calories: 363; Fat: 23 g.; Saturated fat: 3.5 g.

*T*his traditional dish was contributed to Indian cuisine by the Parsee community. Traditionally, the fish, with a chutney made of cilantro and coconut, is wrapped in a banana leaf, then steamed. The banana leaf imparts a distinctive flavor. I have used cabbage leaves and omitted the coconut in this version.

8	large leaves of Savoy cabbage
4	salmon steaks, halved
2–3	tomatoes, sliced, to garnish

Chutney

1 oz.	blanched almonds
1 oz.	sunflower seeds
4½ fl. oz.	boiling water
1 oz.	fresh cilantro leaves and stalks, coarsely chopped
1–2	green chilies, seeded and coarsely chopped
2	large garlic cloves, coarsely chopped
1-inch	cube of fresh ginger, coarsely chopped
1½ tablespoons	lemon juice
½ teaspoon	salt or to taste
1 teaspoon	sugar

➜ For the chutney, soak the almonds and sunflower seeds in the hot water for 10–15 minutes.

+ Meanwhile, blanch the cabbage leaves in boiling salted water for 5 minutes. Drain and refresh in cold water, then drain again and pat dry with paper towels. Carefully cut out and discard the hard stalks from the base of each leaf.

+ Put all the remaining ingredients for the chutney in a blender or food processor. Add the almonds and sunflower seeds, along with the water in which they were soaked, and process until smooth. Divide the chutney into 8 equal portions.

+ Spread half a portion of chutney on a piece of fish and place it, chutney-side down, on a cabbage leaf. Spread the remainder of the portion of chutney on top. Carefully wrap the leaf around the fish to make a neat parcel and tie it up with kitchen string, crisscrossing it around the parcel and making sure there are no gaps. Repeat with the remaining fish, cabbage, and chutney.

+ Prepare a steamer over a saucepan of boiling water. Place the prepared parcels in the steamer and steam for 15 minutes.

+ To serve, carefully remove the string from the parcels and garnish with the sliced tomatoes. Serve immediately.

Note:

Savory Potato Mash (see page 197) or Spiced Sweet Potatoes (see page 200) are delicious with these parcels. Alternatively, serve with Fried Brown Rice (see page 177) and Lentils with Hot Oil Seasoning (see page 168).

Fish in Tamarind Juice
Imli ki Machchi

SERVINGS: 4
PREPARATION TIME: 10–15 minutes
COOKING TIME: 20 minutes
PER SERVING: Calories: 585; Fat: 46 g.; Saturated fat: 14 g.

This recipe is adapted from one of my late mother-in-law's wonderful creations, a dish typical of the southern coastal district of Karnataka.

5½ fl. oz.	reduced-fat coconut milk
5½ fl. oz.	water
½ teaspoon	ground turmeric
1–1¼ teaspoons	chili powder
½ teaspoon	concentrated tamarind pulp or 1 tablespoon tamarind juice (see page 12)
½–1 teaspoon	salt
2 lbs.	mackerel fillets

Hot Oil Seasoning

1 tablespoon	sunflower or canola oil
2 teaspoons	Garlic Purée (see page 16)
1 tablespoon	ground coriander
6–8	fresh or dried curry leaves

✦ Pour the coconut milk and water into a large saucepan, about 12 inches in diameter.

✦ Add the turmeric, chili powder, tamarind, and salt. Bring to a slow simmer and cook, uncovered, for 5 minutes. Stir to dissolve the tamarind.

✦ Meanwhile, cut each mackerel fillet across into 3 pieces. Add to the sauce.

✦ When the sauce bubbles, reduce the heat to low and simmer for 6–8 minutes.

✦ During the last 3–4 minutes of cooking time for the fish, prepare the hot oil seasoning. Heat the oil in a small saucepan over low heat. Add the garlic purée and cook gently for 1 minute, then add the coriander and curry leaves. Cook for 30 seconds before adding the mixture to the fish curry.

→ Shake the pan gently from side to side to ensure that the seasoning is evenly distributed. Serve immediately with boiled basmati rice and Spiced Green Beans (see page 212) or Dry-Spiced Okra (see page 202).

COOK'S TIP: Concentrated tamarind looks and behaves like molasses when you measure it out. It will slide off a lightly greased spoon easily.

Healthy Hint
Mackerel is rich in omega-3 fatty acids,
which are beneficial to the heart.

Tandoori-Style Fish
Tandoori Machchi

SERVINGS: 2
PREPARATION TIME: 15–20 minutes, plus marinating
COOKING TIME: 12–15 minutes
PER SERVING: Calories: 226; Fat: 8.7 g.; Saturated fat: 1.3 g.

*F*ish and seafood cooked in a tandoor (clay oven) take on a characteristic flavor and appearance. Tandoori recipes are great for barbecuing or they can be cooked in a very hot oven or under the grill until the food is slightly charred, when they look very similar to the authentic dish. However, it is hard to replicate the flavors achieved by the tandoori combination of clay and charcoal cooking. In India, the most popular fish for tandoori cooking is pomfret, a firm-fleshed fish found in the Arabian sea. Lemon sole, plaice (a type of flounder), and trout also work very well.

2	rainbow trout, cleaned, with heads and tails attached
1 tablespoon	lemon juice
1/2 teaspoon	salt
2 oz.	modified low-fat plain yogurt (see page 10)
2 teaspoons	Ginger Purée (see page 17)
2 teaspoons	Garlic Purée (see page 16)
1/2 teaspoon	sugar
1/2 teaspoon	ground aniseed
1/2 teaspoon	ground turmeric
1/2 teaspoon	Garam Masala (see page 23)
1/2 teaspoon	chili powder
2 teaspoons	besan (gram or chickpea flour)
1 tablespoon	finely chopped fresh cilantro leaves
1/2	green chili, seeded and finely chopped

Garnish with . . .

sliced scallions, shredded lettuce leaves, and lemon wedges.

➔ Make 3 or 4 diagonal slits on both sides of each fish. Gently rub the lemon juice and salt into the fish. Place in a large shallow dish and set aside for 15–20 minutes.

➔ Place the remaining ingredients, except the cilantro and green chili, in a mixing bowl and beat with a wire whisk until smooth.

➔ Pour the mixture over the fish and rub it gently into them, making sure you rub the mixture into the slits and the stomach cavity. Cover and marinate in the refrigerator for 2–3 hours.

➔ Preheat the grill on high for 10 minutes. Line a grill pan (without the rack) with aluminum foil and brush it lightly with oil.

➔ Place the fish on the foil and cook 3 inches away from the heat source for 6–7 minutes or until slightly charred. Turn the fish over and continue to cook for an additional 5–6 minutes or until charred on the second side.

➔ Add the cilantro and chili to the cooking juices in the grill pan and spoon them over the fish. Transfer to serving plates and add the garnishing ingredients.

➔ Serve immediately, with a raita and any bread to complete the meal.

Chicken Dishes

CHICKEN IS LOWER in fat than other types of meat and the modest amount of fat it does contain is unsaturated, so it is the ideal meat for a low-fat diet. Chicken is also a good source of minerals, some B vitamins, and protein. Thigh meat has plenty of zinc, which is necessary for the efficient functioning of the immune system and essential for growth and reproduction.

The highest fat content in chicken is in the skin and in Indian cooking the skin is always removed. Removing the skin also allows the flavors of spices and other ingredients to penetrate deeper. The use of yogurt, milk, and fruit juices in cooking tenderizes the meat by breaking up the muscle fibers. This further enhances the flavor and texture of the finished dish.

You can buy skinned chicken, but this can be expensive, and it isn't really difficult to skin chicken. The majority of recipes call for chicken thighs or breasts and these are easier to skin than a whole chicken. Use a cloth to hold the skin as you pull it back off the flesh as this prevents slipping, making the task easier and quicker. I have a "meat cloth" that I use specifically for this task—I wash it with normal detergent immediately after I use it and also rinse it in a gentle bleach solution before I thoroughly rinse it in clean water. When it is completely dry, I store it in a plastic bag, sealed with a wire tie, so it is ready for use next time.

Turkey is also low in fat and I have included one turkey recipe in this section; you can use turkey breast in other recipes, instead of chicken, if you like.

Cooking temperature is very important and gentle heat is the key to successful meat and poultry cooking. Once the chicken is tender, you can reduce the sauce, if necessary, by turning the heat up. Remove the meat from the sauce and keep it hot while you reduce the sauce to the required consistency.

Unless otherwise stated, the dishes in this section can be frozen. Make sure you cool the dish quickly by transferring it to a cooling tray (a large roasting pan is ideal). Once cooled, transfer it to a suitable freezer container, then label and chill it before placing in the freezer. Always thaw frozen dishes slowly in the refrigerator, and reheat them gently, but thoroughly, to ensure that the food is piping hot. You may have to add a little warm water occasionally during reheating to prevent a sauce from becoming too dry.

For dry dishes, which do not have a sauce, thaw them as above, then wrap in double-thick foil and place in a preheated oven at 350°F. until completely reheated—allow 15–30 minutes, depending on the type and size of dish.

Chicken in Lentil Sauce
MURGH DHANSAK

SERVINGS: 4
PREPARATION TIME: 25 minutes, plus soaking
COOKING TIME: 1 hour, 15 minutes
PER SERVING: Calories: 355; Fat: 10 g.; Saturated fat: 3 g.

In the 13th century a group of Persians fled their country to avoid religious persecution and they landed on the West Coast of India, now the state of Gujarat, and contributed their culinary influence to the diverse cooking of India. For dhansak, probably the best-loved dish from Western India, the meat is always cooked with lentils and vegetables. *Dhan* means rice and *sak* is vegetable, and Fried Brown Rice (see page 177) is the traditional accompaniment.

Dhal

2 oz.	masoor dhal (red lentils)
2 oz.	toor dhal (yellow split lentils, see page 12)
2 oz.	moong dhal (skinless split mung beans, see page 10)
1	small eggplant, about 8 oz.
½ teaspoon	ground turmeric
1–2	green chilies, seeded and chopped
2-inch	piece of cinnamon stick, halved
½ teaspoon	salt or to taste

Spice mix

1 tablespoon	coriander seeds
1½ teaspoons	cumin seeds
1-inch	piece of cinnamon stick, halved
10–12	black peppercorns
	seeds from 1 brown and 6 green cardamom pods
1–2	dried red chilies, chopped

Chicken

8	boneless chicken thighs, skinned and halved
2 oz.	low-fat plain yogurt
2 teaspoons	Ginger Purée (see page 17)
2 teaspoons	Garlic Purée (see page 16)
½ teaspoon	ground turmeric
1 teaspoon	paprika
1	large onion, finely chopped
6 oz.	tomatoes, chopped
1 teaspoon	dried fenugreek leaves
1 teaspoon	salt or to taste
1 teaspoon	sugar
2½ fl. oz.	warm water
1½ tablespoons	tamarind juice
2–3 tablespoons	chopped fresh cilantro leaves

➔ Wash the masoor dhal, toor dhal, and moong dhal in cold water until the water runs clear, then place in a bowl, cover with plenty of cold water and soak for 30 minutes.

➔ Meanwhile, quarter the eggplant lengthwise and cut into 2-inch pieces. Halve the wider ends, if necessary, before cutting them into pieces. Place in a bowl, cover with cold water to prevent discoloration, and leave to soak until required.

➔ Prepare the spice mix. Preheat a small frying pan over medium heat. Add all the spices, except the chilies, then reduce the heat to low and stir for about 1 minute, until the spices release their aroma. Turn off the heat and add the chilies. Stir for 30 seconds, then transfer the spices to a plate and cool slightly before grinding to a fine powder in a coffee or spice mill. Set aside.

➔ Drain the lentils and eggplant and place in a saucepan. Add 2 cups water and bring to a boil. Reduce the heat to medium, add the turmeric, chilies and cinnamon stick, and cook, uncovered, for 5–6 minutes. Reduce the heat to low, cover the pan and simmer for 25 minutes, stirring occasionally.

➔ Add the salt to the dhal, then set aside to cool until just hot. Discard the cinnamon, and purée the dhal in a blender or press it through a sieve. Set aside.

➔ Put the chicken in a nonstick saucepan and add the yogurt, ginger and garlic purées, turmeric, paprika, and onion. Place over a high heat and stir until the chicken begins to sizzle. Cook for 4–5 minutes, stirring frequently.

➔ Reduce the heat to low, cover the pan, and cook for 10 minutes. Remove the lid and cook, stirring frequently, for 6–7 minutes over medium-high heat until most of the liquid has evaporated.

✦ Reduce the heat to low. Add the ground spices and cook for 2–3 minutes, stirring. Stir in the tomatoes, fenugreek leaves, salt, and sugar, and cook for an additional 2–3 minutes.

✦ Pour the cooked lentil sauce and water into the chicken. Reduce the heat to low, cover the pan and cook for 15 minutes or until the chicken is tender. Stir regularly to ensure that the thickened sauce doesn't stick to the pan, adding a little extra water if necessary.

✦ Stir in the tamarind juice and cilantro, then serve with Fried Brown Rice (see page 177).

Chicken in Yogurt
DAHI MURGH

SERVINGS: 4
PREPARATION TIME: 15 minutes
COOKING TIME: 45–50 minutes
PER SERVING: Calories: 240; Fat: 9 g.; Saturated fat: 3 g.

*T*his dish is adapted from a traditional recipe. Cooking chicken gently in yogurt without any additional liquid results in a delicious, concentrated flavor.

1	large onion, finely sliced
1 teaspoon	salt or to taste
2 teaspoons	Ginger Purée (see page 17)
2 teaspoons	Garlic Purée (see page 16)
½ teaspoon	ground turmeric
½–1 teaspoon	chili powder
2 teaspoons	Ground Roasted Coriander (see page 22)
1½ teaspoons	Ground Roasted Cumin (see page 21)
4½ oz.	low-fat plain yogurt
8	chicken thighs, skinned
1 teaspoon	sugar
2 1-inch	pieces of cinnamon stick
4	green cardamom pods, bruised
4	whole cloves
1 tablespoon	tomato purée
½ teaspoon	Garam Masala (see page 23)
2 tablespoons	chopped fresh cilantro leaves

➔ Cook the onion and salt in a nonstick saucepan over low heat for 2–3 minutes. Increase the heat to medium and continue cooking, stirring frequently, for an additional 2–3 minutes or until the onion is soft. The salt draws out the natural juices from the onions, so that they can be cooked without added fat and without burning. Reduce the heat slightly toward the end of cooking, if necessary.

→ Stir in the ginger and garlic purées, turmeric, chili powder, coriander, and cumin. Cook for 1 minute, then add half the yogurt to moisten the spices. Stir and cook for an additional minute.

→ Add the chicken, sugar, cinnamon, cardamoms, cloves, and the remaining yogurt. Stir to mix thoroughly, then cover the pan, reduce the heat to low, and cook for 35–40 minutes, stirring occasionally.

→ Stir in the tomato purée, garam masala, and cilantro, and simmer for 2–3 minutes. Serve with boiled basmati rice or Fried Brown Rice (see page 177) and Cabbage Salad (see page 230).

Chicken in Milk
MURGH SHAFAK SHEER

SERVINGS: 4
PREPARATION TIME: 15 minutes, plus cooling the spices
COOKING TIME: 40–45 minutes
PER SERVING: Calories: 261; Fat: 10 g.; Saturated fat: 3 g.

I have adapted this recipe for healthy eating from a rather exotic dish created in the style of the Indian Royal House of Sailana. In his book, *Cooking Delights of the Maharajas,* Maharaja Digvijaya Singh gives an insight into this fascinating style of cooking. I have omitted ghee and used chicken instead of mutton for my version, which is less rich than the Maharaja's opulent creation, but retains much of its fabulous flavor.

2 teaspoons	coriander seeds
1½ teaspoons	cumin seeds
½ teaspoon	black peppercorns
2–4	dried red chilies, chopped
1 tablespoon	sunflower seeds
1½ lbs.	boneless chicken breasts or thighs, skinned
2 teaspoons	Ginger Purée (see page 17)
2 teaspoons	Garlic Purée (see page 16)
1	large onion, finely sliced
2 1-inch	pieces of cinnamon stick
6	green cardamom pods, bruised
1 teaspoon	salt or to taste
½ teaspoon	ground turmeric
2 teaspoons	besan (gram or chickpea flour)
10 fl. oz.	hot 2% milk
2 tablespoons	chopped cilantro

+ Preheat a small frying pan over medium heat for about 1 minute. Reduce the heat to low and add the coriander seeds, cumin seeds, peppercorns, chilies, and sunflower seeds. Roast the spices for 1 minute or until they release their aroma. Transfer to a plate and cool, then grind the spices to a fine powder in a coffee or spice mill.

+ Cut the chicken breasts into 2-inch cubes or halve the thighs, and put them in a heavy nonstick saucepan, at least 12 inches in diameter. Add the ginger and garlic purées, the onion, cinnamon, cardamoms, and salt. Cook over high heat, stirring, for 5–6 minutes or until the chicken begins to brown.

+ Reduce the heat to low-medium, cover the pan and cook for 15 minutes, stirring at least twice. Remove the lid and increase the heat to medium-high, then cook, stirring frequently, until the liquid reduces and thickens to a paste.

+ Add the ground spices and turmeric. Cook for an additional 2–3 minutes, stirring constantly, until the chicken is well browned.

+ Blend the besan with a little water to make a thin paste and strain it through a fine sieve into the milk, pushing through any tiny lumps that form. Stir well, then pour over the chicken and reduce the heat to low. Cover the pan tightly and cook for 15–20 minutes or until the sauce has thickened and the chicken is tender.

+ Stir in the cilantro and remove from the heat. Serve with Saffron Rice (see page 176), accompanied by a raita or vegetable dish, such as Leeks with Coconut (see page 214).

Chicken in Apricot Juice

MURGH KHUBANI

SERVINGS: 6
PREPARATION TIME: 20–25 minutes, plus marinating
COOKING TIME: 35–40 minutes
PER SERVING: Calories: 330 g.; Fat: 8 g.; Saturated fat: 3 g.

A gorgeous dish from Kashmir with a sweet, savory and tangy-hot flavor. Kashmir is noted for its exquisite fruits and flowers, and Kashmiri chefs are highly prized throughout the country for their skill and talent in producing fabulous dishes with local produce. Although cooked without fat, this version of a famous chicken dish is every bit as delicious as the original.

6	boneless chicken breasts, about 2¼ lbs., skinned
4 oz.	low-fat plain yogurt
2 teaspoons	Ginger Purée (see page 17)
2 teaspoons	Garlic Purée (see page 16)
5–6	shallots, finely chopped
1 teaspoon	Roasted Ground Cumin (see page 21)
2 teaspoons	Roasted Ground Coriander (see page 22)
½–1 teaspoon	chili powder
12	ready-to-eat dried apricots
14 fl. oz.	hot water
1–2	green chilies, seeded and coarsely chopped
1 teaspoon	salt or to taste
½ teaspoon	sugar
¼ teaspoon	ground cardamom
¼ teaspoon	ground nutmeg
3 fl. oz.	fat-free half-and-half
2 tablespoons	chopped fresh cilantro

- Cut each chicken breast diagonally into 2–3 chunky pieces. In a large bowl, blend the remaining ingredients up to and including the chili powder. Add the chicken and mix well, then cover and place in refrigerator to marinate for 3–4 hours. If you wish, you can leave the chicken to marinate overnight in the refrigerator, but bring it to room temperature before cooking.
- Roughly chop the apricots and soak them in 5 fl. oz. of the hot water for 15 minutes, then purée them in a blender with the chilies. Set aside.
- Put the marinated chicken in a nonstick saucepan, at least 12 inches in diameter, and place over medium-high heat. Cook for 3–4 minutes, stirring, until the chicken changes color and begins to release its juices. Cover the pan, reduce the heat to low and simmer for 15 minutes. Remove the lid and increase the heat to high. Cook for 10–12 minutes or until all the liquid evaporates, reducing the heat to medium towards the last 1–2 minutes.
- Add the apricot purée, salt, sugar, and remaining hot water. Mix well, cover and simmer for 6–7 minutes. Add the cardamom and nutmeg and cook, uncovered, for 5 minutes over medium heat. Stir in the half-and-half and cilantro and remove from the heat.
- Serve with boiled basmati rice or any bread, accompanied by a dry-spiced vegetable dish, such as Carrots and Green Beans with Poppy Seeds (see page 204).

COOK'S TIP: If the yogurt curdles in step 3, add 2 teaspoons besan (gram or chickpea flour) blended with a little water.

Chicken in Coconut Milk

NARIYAL KI MURGH

SERVINGS: 4
PREPARATION TIME: 20–25 minutes
COOKING TIME: 35–40 minutes
PER SERVING: Calories: 325; Fat: 12 g.; Saturated fat: 6 g.

To accent the rich flavor of coconut milk without all the saturated fat that it contains, equal portions of reduced-fat coconut milk and water have been used in all the recipes, including the following dish. The absence of any other added fat gives this entrée a light and refreshing flavor.

2 lbs.	chicken breasts or thighs, skinned
1	large onion, finely chopped
1 tablespoon	Garlic Purée (see page 16)
1 tablespoon	Ginger Purée (see page 17)
2 oz.	low-fat plain yogurt
½ teaspoon	ground turmeric
2 teaspoons	Ground Roasted Coriander (see page 22)
1 teaspoon	Ground Roasted Cumin (see page 21)
½–1 teaspoon	chili powder
1 teaspoon	salt or to taste
5 fl. oz.	reduced-fat coconut milk
5 fl. oz.	water
4	green chilies, with the stalks intact
8–10	curry leaves
½ teaspoon	Garam Masala (see page 23)
1 tablespoon	lemon juice

➤ If using chicken breasts, use poultry scissors or a meat cleaver to chop the joints into two smaller portions. Thighs can be left whole. Put the chicken into a nonstick saucepan, at least 12 inches in diameter, and add the onion, garlic and ginger purées, and yogurt. Mix thoroughly, then cover the pan. Cook over medium heat, until the contents begin to bubble. Reduce the heat to low and stir the chicken once, then cover and cook for 20 minutes, stirring occasionally.

→ Increase the heat to high and cook the chicken, uncovered, until the liquid has reduced and thickened slightly, then reduce the heat to medium. The chicken will have now released its natural fat. Add the turmeric, coriander and cumin, the chili powder and salt.

→ Cook, stirring constantly, until the sauce is reduced to a paste-like consistency and the fat from the chicken is clearly visible—this will take 4–5 minutes.

→ Blend the coconut milk and water, then add to the chicken with the fresh chilies, curry leaves, and garam masala. Simmer, uncovered, for 6–8 minutes. Stir in the lemon juice and remove from the heat.

→ Serve immediately, with boiled basmati rice and Spinach Raita (see page 222) or Cauliflower with Green Chutney (see page 208).

COOK'S TIP: The chicken is left on the bone for extra flavor. If you want to cook boneless meat, then add 8 oz. bones to the pan and remove them before serving the dish. Alternatively, use Aromatic Stock (see page 25).

Chicken with Chili and Lime
Mirchi aur Nimbuwali Murgh

SERVINGS: 4
PREPARATION TIME: 20 minutes
COOKING TIME: 30 minutes
PER SERVING: Calories: 96; Fat: 7 g.; Saturated fat: 2.25 g.

This dish has an attractive, fresh appearance with an aroma and flavor to match. Chili and lime is a combination that's hard to beat. Don't be alarmed by the quantity and variety of chili used here—the powdered chili complements the tart limes and the fresh chilies are seeded to reduce their pungency. You can further reduce their hot flavor by soaking the slit chilies in cold water for 15–20 minutes, then rinsing them well.

1 lb., 2 oz.	boneless chicken thighs, skinned and halved
	juice of 2 limes
2 teaspoons	Ginger Purée (see page 17)
2 teaspoons	Garlic Purée (see page 16)
1	large onion, finely chopped
½ teaspoon	ground turmeric
1 teaspoon	Ground Roasted Cumin (see page 21)
2 teaspoons	Ground Roasted Coriander (see page 22)
½–1 teaspoon	chili powder
1 teaspoon	salt or to taste
1½ teaspoons	sugar
8 oz.	Boiled Onion Purée (see page 18)
7 fl. oz.	warm water
2 tablespoons	chopped fresh cilantro leaves
1–2	green chilies, seeded and cut into julienne strips
2	red chilies, seeded and cut into julienne strips
½ teaspoon	Garam Masala (see page 23)

→ Put the chicken into a nonstick saucepan, at least 10 inches in diameter, and add the lime juice, ginger and garlic purées, chopped onion, and turmeric. Stir to mix thoroughly. Place the pan over medium heat and cook gently until the contents begin to bubble, then cover and cook for 10–12 minutes over medium-low heat, stirring occasionally. At the end of this time, the chicken will have released its juices.

→ Remove the lid and increase the heat slightly. Cook the chicken until the juices are reduced to a thick paste—this will take 4–5 minutes. Stir frequently to ensure that the thickened paste doesn't stick to the bottom of the pan.

→ Add the cumin, ground coriander, chili powder, salt, and sugar. Reduce the heat to medium and continue to cook for an additional 1–2 minutes, stirring constantly.

→ Add half the onion purée and cook, stirring frequently, for 3–4 minutes or until the onion purée is dry enough to coat the pieces of chicken. Repeat with the remaining onion purée and warm water, then cook, uncovered, for 4–5 minutes or until the sauce has thickened.

→ Reserve a little of the fresh cilantro and each variety of chilies for garnish and add the remainder to the chicken along with the garam masala. Stir well to distribute the ingredients and remove the pan from the heat. Garnish with the reserved cilantro and chilies, and serve with Tandoori Bread (see page 192) or Chapatis (see page 188) and Cucumber and Peanut Salad (see page 231).

Chicken Korma

MURGH KORMA

SERVINGS: 4
PREPARATION TIME: 15–20 minutes
COOKING TIME: 35 minutes
PER SERVING: Calories: 280; Fat: 10 g.; Saturated fat: 3 g.

*I*n the West, korma has come to represent a very mild dish that is drowned in cream, but authentically, it is the Indian term for braising. A korma can be mild or rather fiery, depending on regional variations: for example, in the south a korma is enriched with coconut milk and plenty of chilies are added to counteract the sweetness. Korma is Mogul in origin and, in the north, where the Moguls established themselves, there are many versions of this popular dish, usually with rich ingredients like saffron, nuts, khoya (full-fat dried milk), and cream. This recipe is a healthy variation on a northern korma.

1 oz.	unroasted cashew nut pieces
pinch	saffron threads
2 fl. oz.	boiling water
1 lb.	boneless chicken breasts or thighs, skinned
2 oz.	low-fat plain yogurt
1	large onion, finely chopped
6	green cardamom pods, bruised
2	1-inch pieces of cinnamon stick
4	cloves
1 tablespoon	Ginger Purée (see page 17)
1 tablespoon	Garlic Purée (see page 16)
1 teaspoon	salt or to taste
½ teaspoon	ground turmeric
½–1 teaspoon	chili powder
½ teaspoon	ground white pepper
1 tablespoon	Ground Roasted Coriander (see page 22)
10 fl. oz.	Aromatic Stock (see page 25)

4 oz.	Browned Onion Purée (see page 20)
2 tablespoons	fat-free half-and-half
½ teaspoon	Garam Masala (see page 23)
1 tablespoon	low-fat sour cream
½ teaspoon	paprika

✦ Put the cashews and saffron in a bowl and pour in the boiling water. Leave to soak for 15–20 minutes.

✦ Meanwhile, cut the chicken breasts into 2-inch cubes or halve the thighs. Put the chicken in a nonstick saucepan, at least 10 inches in diameter. Add the yogurt, chopped onion, cardamoms, cinnamon, cloves, and ginger and garlic purées. Mix thoroughly and place over medium heat, then cover and cook for 5–6 minutes.

✦ Stir the chicken, reduce the heat to low and cook, covered, for an additional 5–7 minutes. Remove the lid and increase the heat to medium-high, then cook, stirring frequently, for 6–8 minutes or until the liquid evaporates to form a thick paste.

✦ Add the salt, turmeric, chili powder, pepper, and coriander, and cook, stirring frequently, for 3–4 minutes or until the chicken begins to brown. Stir in the stock and onion purée. Cover and cook over low heat for 8–10 minutes.

✦ Meanwhile, purée the cashews, saffron, and their soaking water in a blender. Add the half-and-half and process until smooth. Pour this over the chicken. Add the garam masala and cook, uncovered, for 2–3 minutes.

✦ Transfer the korma to a serving dish. Swirl the low-fat sour cream over the top and sprinkle with the paprika. Serve immediately, with Saffron Rice (see page 176) and Carrots and Green Beans with Poppy Seeds (see page 204).

COOK'S TIP: If you do not have time to make the stock, add 8 oz. chicken bones and remove them before serving the dish.

COOK'S TIP: To make this dish a little spicier, try adding two-thirds paprika and one-third hot chili powder.

Chicken Do-Piaza
DO-PIAZA MURGH

SERVINGS: 4
PREPARATION TIME: 20 minutes
COOKING TIME: 30 minutes
PER SERVING: Calories: 244; Fat: 9 g.; Saturated fat: 3 g.

*T*he meaning of the word *do-piaza* remains controversial: *do* means two or twice and *piaz* is onion. Therefore, some believe the name refers to the amount of onions used in the recipe (twice the norm), while others insist that the name comes from the equal quantities of onions and meat, which were used in the original recipe. The third and more reasonable explanation is that the dish was named after the Mogul Emperor Akbar's courtier, Mullah Dopiaza.

8	boneless chicken thighs, skinned and halved
2 teaspoons	Ginger Purée (see page 17)
2 teaspoons	Garlic Purée (see page 16)
2 2-inch	pieces of cinnamon stick, halved
2	brown cardamom pods, bruised
4	cloves
2	bay leaves, crumbled
1	large red onion, halved and finely sliced
½ teaspoon	ground turmeric
½–1 teaspoon	chili powder
1 teaspoon	Ground Roasted Cumin (see page 21)
1 teaspoon	Ground Roasted Coriander (see page 22)
2 tablespoons	low-fat plain yogurt
8 oz.	Boiled Onion Purée (see page 18)
1 teaspoon	salt or to taste
1 tablespoon	tomato purée
10 fl. oz.	Aromatic Stock (see page 25)
1	large tomato, cut into chunks

| 2–4 | green chilies, with the stalks intact |
| 2–3 tablespoons | chopped fresh cilantro leaves |

→ Put the chicken in a heavy nonstick saucepan, at least 12 inches in diameter, and add the ginger and garlic purées, cinnamon, cardamoms, cloves and bay leaves. Cook over medium-high heat for 7–8 minutes, stirring, until the chicken begins to brown.

→ Reduce the heat slightly, add the red onion, and continue to cook for 3–4 minutes, stirring frequently.

→ Add the turmeric, chili powder, cumin, and coriander, and cook for 1 minute. Add half the yogurt and cook for 2–3 minutes, then repeat with the remaining yogurt. Add the onion purée and continue to cook for 3–4 minutes, stirring.

→ Stir in the salt, tomato purée, and stock, and bring to a boil. Reduce the heat to low and cook, uncovered, for 12–15 minutes. Stir occasionally to ensure that the thickened sauce doesn't stick to the pan.

→ Add the tomato, chilies, and fresh cilantro. Cook for 1 minute, then serve with Tandoori Bread (see page 192) and a raita.

COOK'S TIP: Do not remove the stalks from the green chilies unless you like your food hot. Once the stalk is removed, the chili will release its juices into the sauce, making it hot.

Chili Chicken
Murgh aur Mirchi

Servings: 4
Preparation time: 20 minutes, plus marinating
Cooking time: 25–30 minutes
Per serving: Calories: 240; Fat: 9 g.; Saturated fat: 3 g.

This is a fairly dry dish, cooked by the bhuna method, which is a form of stir-frying. When finished, the sauce is reduced to a thick paste that coats the chicken. Strips of red and green chili and coarse-cut cilantro make the chicken look irresistibly yummy, and it tastes delicious with any bread and a chutney or raita.

8	boneless chicken thighs, skinned and halved
2 tablespoons	lemon juice
1 teaspoon	salt or to taste
2 teaspoons	Ginger Purée (see page 17)
2 teaspoons	Garlic Purée (see page 16)
½ teaspoon	ground turmeric
½–1 teaspoon	chili powder
1 teaspoon	Ground Roasted Coriander (see page 22)
1 teaspoon	Ground Roasted Cumin (see page 21)
10 oz.	Browned Onion Purée (see page 20)
1½ teaspoons	sugar
8 oz.	tomatoes, finely chopped
2½ fl oz.	warm water
1–2	red chilies, seeded and cut into julienne strips
1–2	green chilies, seeded and cut into julienne strips
½ teaspoon	Garam Masala (see page 23)
2–3 tablespoons	coarsely chopped fresh cilantro leaves

✦ Put the chicken in a large bowl and rub the lemon juice and salt into the pieces. Set aside for 30 minutes.

✦ Put the chicken in a nonstick saucepan, at least 12 inches in diameter and add the ginger and garlic purées. Cook over medium heat, stirring, until sizzling. Increase the heat to high and cook for 2–3 minutes, stirring constantly.

✦ Add the turmeric, chili powder, ground coriander, and cumin, and reduce the heat to medium. Cook for 2 minutes, stirring constantly.

✦ Stir in half the onion purée and cook for 4–5 minutes, stirring occasionally, then add the remaining onion purée and sugar. Continue to cook for an additional 4–5 minutes, stirring frequently.

✦ Add the tomatoes and the water, mix well, and cover the pan tightly.

✦ Reduce the heat to low and cook for 10 minutes.

✦ Remove the lid and increase the heat to medium. Continue to cook for 3–4 minutes, stirring frequently, then add the red and green chilies and garam masala. Cook for 4–5 minutes or until the sauce has thickened.

✦ Finally, stir in the cilantro and cook for 1 minute. Remove from the heat and serve immediately.

COOK'S TIP: Removing the seeds from the chilies will reduce their pungency. If you want to reduce the heat further, soak the strips in cold water until required. Drain well before adding to the dish.

Dry-Spiced Chicken Drumsticks

SUKHA MASALEKI TANGRI

SERVINGS: 4
PREPARATION TIME: 15 minutes
COOKING TIME: 25 minutes
PER SERVING: Calories: 215; Fat: 9 g.; Saturated fat: 3 g.

Here, a simple cooking method contributes fabulous aroma and taste to a dish that makes a good mid-week family meal or can be served as a side dish on a dinner-party menu.

8	chicken drumsticks, skinned
2 teaspoons	Garlic Purée (see page 16)
2 teaspoons	Ginger Purée (see page 17)
½–1 teaspoon	salt or to taste
2 oz.	low-fat plain yogurt
2 teaspoons	Ground Roasted Coriander (see page 22)
1 teaspoons	Ground Roasted Cumin (see page 21)
½–1 teaspoon	chili powder
½ teaspoon	ground turmeric
10 fl. oz.	warm water
1 teaspoon	Garam Masala (see page 23)
3 oz.	canned chopped tomatoes, with their juice
2 tablespoons	chopped fresh cilantro leaves
1 tablespoon	chopped fresh mint or ½ teaspoon dried mint

→ Put the chicken drumsticks in a nonstick saucepan, at least 12 inches in diameter, and add the garlic and ginger purées, salt, yogurt, ground coriander, cumin, chili powder, turmeric, and water. Bring to a boil over medium heat. Cover and reduce the heat to low. Cook for 20 minutes, stirring occasionally.

→ Remove the lid and increase the heat to high. Cook the drumsticks for 2–3 minutes or until the sauce thickens slightly, stirring frequently.

→ Reduce the heat to medium. Add the garam masala, tomatoes, fresh coriander, and mint. Stir and cook until the sauce resembles a thick paste. Remove from the heat and serve with soft, puffy Chapatis (see page 188) and a raita or Spiced Sweet Potatoes (see page 200).

COOK'S TIP: For a cook-ahead meal, cook to the end of the first step, then cool and chill overnight or for up to 2 days. Complete the cooking process just before serving.

Chicken in Green Sauce

HARIYALI MURGH

SERVINGS: 4
PREPARATION TIME: 15 minutes
COOKING TIME: 25–30 minutes
PER SERVING: Calories: 225; Fat: 9 g.; Saturated fat: 3 g.

This is a super, quick dish with fabulous flavor. The chicken is cooked in a green spice paste without added stock or water. Traditionally, ghee or oil is added to fry the chicken at the end of the cooking time, but this light version is delicious without the added fat.

1 oz.	fresh cilantro leaves and stalks, coarsely chopped
15–20	fresh mint leaves
4	large garlic cloves, chopped
1-inch	cube of fresh ginger, peeled and coarsely chopped
1–2	green chilies, seeded and chopped
1	onion, coarsely chopped
2	tomatoes, about 4½ oz. in total, skinned and chopped
2 oz.	low-fat plain yogurt
½ teaspoon	chili powder
2 teaspoons	Ground Roasted Coriander (see page 22)
4	green cardamom pods, bruised
8	boneless chicken thighs, skinned and halved or 1½ lbs. boneless chicken breasts, skinned and cut into 2-inch cubes
1 teaspoon	salt or to taste

→ Purée the coriander, mint, garlic, ginger, chilies, onion, tomatoes, and yogurt in a blender. Pour into a nonstick saucepan, at least 12 inches in diameter.

→ Add the remaining ingredients, except the salt, and place the pan over high heat. Cook, stirring, for 4–5 minutes or until the chicken turns opaque. Reduce the heat to low, cover the pan, and cook for 20–25 minutes.

→ Stir in the salt and cook, uncovered, over medium heat for 8–10 minutes or until the sauce has reduced and resembles a thick paste.

→ Serve with Tandoori Bread (see page 192) and Mixed Vegetable Curry (see page 210) or a Raita.

Chicken Meatballs in a Rich Sauce

MURGH KOFTA SHAHI

SERVINGS: 4
PREPARATION TIME: 35 minutes, plus chilling
COOKING TIME: 35 minutes
PER SERVING: Calories: 334; Fat: 18 g.; Saturated fat: 6.5 g.

These melt-in-your-mouth chicken meatballs are simmered in a korma sauce enriched with cashew nut purée. The dish is equally delicious made with ground turkey.

Meatballs

1 lb.	ground chicken
1 teaspoon	Garam Masala (see page 23)
1	large egg
1–2	green chilies, seeded and coarsely chopped
1/4 oz.	fresh cilantro leaves and stalks
2	large garlic cloves, coarsely chopped
1-inch	cube of fresh ginger, peeled and coarsely chopped
1	small onion, coarsely chopped
1/2 teaspoon	salt or to taste

Sauce

2 oz.	unroasted cashew nut pieces
15 fl. oz.	hot water
1 tablespoon	besan (gram or chickpea flour)
3 oz.	low-fat plain yogurt
1/2–1 teaspoon	chili powder
1/2 teaspoon	ground turmeric
1 teaspoon	paprika
1 teaspoon	Ground Roasted Cumin (see page 21)

1 teaspoon	Ground Roasted Coriander (see page 22)
1 tablespoon	tomato purée
1 teaspoon	salt or to taste
1 teaspoon	sugar
4	green cardamom pods, bruised
2-inch	piece of cinnamon stick, halved
½ teaspoon	Garam Masala (see page 23)
5 fl. oz.	fat-free half-and-half
2 tablespoons	chopped fresh cilantro leaves

→ Put all the ingredients for the meatballs in a food processor and blend until smooth. Transfer to a mixing bowl and cover with plastic wrap, then chill for 30 minutes. If you do not have a food processor, finely chop the chilies, coriander, garlic, ginger and onion (or purée these ingredients in a blender) and mix with the other ingredients by hand until thoroughly combined.

→ Meanwhile, for the sauce, soak the cashew nuts in 5 fl. oz. of the hot water for 20 minutes.

→ Shape the kofta mixture into 16 balls, each about the size of a lime, smoothing them by gently rotating and pressing between the palms of your hands.

→ To make the sauce, sieve the besan and blend it to a smooth paste with a little cold water, then mix in the yogurt, chili powder, turmeric, paprika, cumin, ground coriander, tomato purée, salt, and sugar. Set aside.

→ Use a saucepan large enough to hold the meatballs in a single layer and add the remaining hot water, cardamoms, and cinnamon stick. Heat until simmering, then carefully add the meatballs in a single layer. Cover and cook for 10–12 minutes or until the meatballs are firm enough for the liquid to be stirred.

→ Reduce the heat to low and carefully stir in the besan and spice mixture. Re-cover the pan and cook for 10 minutes.

→ Meanwhile, purée the cashew nuts with the water in which they were soaked and add to the meatballs with the garam masala and half-and-half. Simmer for 5–7 minutes.

→ Stir in the cilantro and serve immediately. Any bread or boiled basmati rice makes a suitable accompaniment with a vegetable dish, such as Cabbage with Ginger (see page 206).

COOK'S TIP: For puréed cashews, buy broken nuts or cashew pieces—they're less expensive.

Chicken in Tomato and Coconut Sauce

Tamatar Aur Nariyal ki Murgh

Servings: 4
Preparation time: 15 minutes
Cooking time: 35 minutes
Per serving: Calories: 260; Fat: 14 g.; Saturated fat: 7 g.

When you are absolutely frantic, this recipe will rescue you time and time again. You simply mix everything together and while the chicken is cooking, boil the rice. There will still be time to make a salad.

1 oz.	desiccated coconut
5 fl. oz.	boiling water
½ oz.	fresh cilantro leaves and stalks
1–2	green chilies, seeded
2	large garlic cloves
1-inch	cube of fresh ginger, peeled and coarsely chopped
8 oz.	passata (see "Cook's Tip" below)
8	chicken thighs, skinned
1 teaspoon	salt or to taste
2 tablespoons	fat-free half-and-half

➔ Soak the coconut in the hot water for 10–15 minutes. Purée the coconut and its soaking water in a blender with the coriander, chilies, garlic, and ginger until smooth.

➔ Put the passata, chicken, and salt in a saucepan, at least 12 inches in diameter, and place over medium heat. When the passata begins to bubble, reduce the heat to low, cover and cook for 20 minutes.

→ Stir in the blended coconut mixture and heat until the sauce begins to bubble again, then cover the pan and cook for 10–12 minutes.

→ Finally, add the half-and-half, cook for 1 minute and serve at once.

 COOK'S TIP: Passata is a thick, sieved tomato purée. Alternatively, use the same amount of canned tomatoes and purée them in a blender or sieve them until smooth.

Chicken Tikka Masala
Murgh Tikka Masala

SERVINGS: 4
PREPARATION TIME: 5 minutes, plus preparing chicken tikka
COOKING TIME: 17–18 minutes, plus cooking chicken tikka
PER SERVING: Calories: 445; Fat: 22 g.; Saturated fat: 10 g.

Chicken tikka is a traditional Indian dish, but masala is a clever invention. In the seventies a masala (spiced) sauce was added to chicken tikka to satisfy a customer who thought the meat was too dry. Now, there is hardly any Indian restaurant in the U.S. that doesn't have CTM (as it is known in the trade) as one of the most popular dishes on the menu. I have even come across this dish in some restaurants in India.

5 fl. oz.	fat-free half-and-half
2 oz.	low-fat sour cream
8½ fl. oz.	Aromatic Stock (see page 25)
½ teaspoon	Ground Roasted Cumin (see page 21)
½ teaspoon	Ground Roasted Coriander (see page 22)
1–2	green chilies, seeded and chopped
1 tablespoon	tomato purée
½ teaspoon	salt or to taste
½ teaspoon	sugar
1	quantity cooked Chicken Tikka (see page 34)
2 tablespoons	finely chopped fresh cilantro leaves

→ Mix all the ingredients, except the cooked chicken tikka and cilantro, in a saucepan and place over medium heat. As soon as the sauce starts bubbling, turn the heat down to low and simmer for 10 minutes.

→ Cool the sauce slightly, then purée it in a blender or press it through a sieve. Return to the saucepan and add the cooked chicken tikka. Simmer for 5 minutes or until the chicken is thoroughly heated.

→ Add the cilantro and simmer for 2–3 minutes. Serve with Tandoori Bread (see page 192) or Cumin-Coriander Rice (see page 174) and a raita.

COOK'S TIP: The chicken tikka can be cooked in advance, cooled, and chilled or frozen with all its cooking juices. Thaw the chicken and, for extra flavor, be sure to add the juices to the sauce at the start of cooking the above recipe.

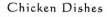

Baked Chicken

DUM KA MURGH

SERVINGS: 4
PREPARATION TIME: 30 minutes, plus marinating
COOKING TIME: 45 minutes
PER SERVING: Calories: 210; Fat: 9 g.; Saturated fat: 2 g.

This is an adaptation of a recipe from Hyderabad, a princely city with forts and palaces in southern India. The last of the Mogul Emperors retired to this city, and the strong tradition of Mogul cooking makes the cuisine of Hyderabad unique among the southern states.

4	chicken joints (attached drumsticks and thighs), skinned
1 tablespoon	lemon juice
1 teaspoon	salt or to taste
½ teaspoon	chili powder
4½ oz.	low-fat plain yogurt
2-inch	cube of fresh ginger, peeled and coarsely chopped
4	garlic cloves, peeled and coarsely chopped
5–6	shallots, coarsely chopped
2 teaspoons	white poppy seeds
1 tablespoon	sunflower seeds
	seeds from 4 green cardamom pods
2	cloves
1-inch	piece of cinnamon stick, broken

Basting sauce

pinch	saffron threads, pounded
2 tablespoons	hot milk
1 tablespoon	finely chopped fresh cilantro leaves
½ teaspoon	dried mint

- ✦ Prick the chicken joints all over with the point of a sharp knife or a fork. Rub the lemon juice, salt, and chili powder into the chicken and set aside.
- ✦ Place the yogurt in a blender and add the ginger, garlic, and shallots. Purée until smooth.
- ✦ In a coffee or spice mill, grind the poppy seeds, sunflower seeds, cardamom seeds, cloves, and cinnamon to a fine powder.
- ✦ Mix the ground spices and yogurt purée, then pour over the chicken joints. Turn the joints and spoon the mixture over them until they're thoroughly coated. Cover and leave to marinate for 3–4 hours in a cool place or overnight in the refrigerator. Bring the chicken to room temperature before cooking.
- ✦ For the basting sauce, soak the saffron threads in the hot milk for 15 minutes, then stir in the coriander and mint. Preheat the oven to 400°F.
- ✦ Line a roasting tin with foil and brush it lightly with oil. Place the chicken and marinade in the tin and bake for 15–20 minutes. Turn the joints over and bake for an additional 15–20 minutes, basting with the pan juices at least twice.
- ✦ Brush some of the basting sauce over the chicken and continue to cook for 3–4 minutes. Turn the joints over and brush with the remaining basting sauce. Cook for a final 2–3 minutes. Serve immediately, with a raita and Chapatis (see page 188) or Karnataka Potato Curry (see page 198).

Spicy Roast Chicken
Masala Tandoori Murgh

SERVINGS: 4
PREPARATION TIME: 25 minutes, plus marinating
COOKING TIME: 45–50 minutes
PER SERVING: Calories: 215; Fat: 6 g.; Saturated fat: 2 g.

Although similar, this isn't quite the same as tandoori chicken. In Indian cooking, a tandoor (clay oven) is used for roasting and it imparts its characteristic flavor to the food. In this recipe, I have modified the process and cooked the chicken in a hot oven. I am delighted with the result because it captures the tandoori flavor as closely as possible. For a special Sunday lunch, serve Vegetable Pilau (see page 186) or Savory Potato Mash (see page 197) and Kohlrabi Salad (see page 232) as accompaniments.

1	roasting chicken, about 3 lbs.
3 oz.	low-fat plain yogurt
1 tablespoon	lemon juice
1 tablespoon	Garlic Purée (see page 16)
1 tablespoon	Ginger Purée (see page 17)
1/2–1 teaspoon	chili powder
1/2–1 teaspoon	salt or to taste
1 teaspoon	Ground Roasted Cumin (see page 21)
1 teaspoon	Ground Roasted Coriander (see page 22)

Garnish with . . .
sprigs of fresh cilantro, 1–2 red chilies (seeded and sliced), and red onion slices.

✤ Skin the chicken: The easiest way to do this is to hold the chicken with one hand and cover the other hand with a clean dishtowel or new disposable dishcloth, then start pulling the skin away from the neck end. Carefully work your way around the thighs and legs right down to the stomach end of the chicken. The cloth prevents slipping and is much easier and quicker than using a knife.

➤ Lay the chicken on a flat surface and make short, deep incisions all over the flesh, including the wings, inside thighs, legs, and back. Remove the pope's nose and wing and leg tips.

➤ Mix all the remaining ingredients, except the cumin and coriander. Rub the mixture well into the chicken, making sure you work the mixture into the incisions. Place the chicken in a deep container, cover, and chill overnight. Bring the chicken to room temperature before cooking.

➤ Preheat the oven to 400°F. Place the marinated chicken in a 12 x 8-inch roasting tin. Spread any remaining marinade on the chicken and roast for 25 minutes.

➤ Pour 3 fl. oz. water into the roasting tin and continue to cook for an additional 20 minutes. Baste the chicken generously with the cooking juices, then cook for an additional 15–20 minutes, basting twice.

➤ Sprinkle the cumin and ground coriander all over the chicken and cook for a final 5 minutes. Baste again with the thickened cooking juices so that the spices cling to the chicken. Transfer to a serving dish.

➤ Strain any remaining cooking juices and pour them over the chicken. Garnish with sprigs of cilantro, sliced chilies, and onion slices, and serve immediately.

Semi-Tandoori Chicken
Adha Tandoori Murgh

SERVINGS: 4
PREPARATION TIME: 15 minutes, plus marinating
COOKING TIME: 25 minutes
PER SERVING: Calories: 180; Fat: 4.5 g.; Saturated fat: 1.5 g.

I christened this dish semi-tandoori as I have used only half the range of spices that are used in classic tandoori chicken. It is a simple recipe, but it has a spectacular taste and appearance, and is simply divine served with Chapatis (see page 188), Savory Potato Mash (see page 197), and Mixed Vegetable Curry (see page 210) with a raita or chutney. Use either chicken leg or breast quarters, or a combination of the two.

4	chicken pieces, skinned
5½ oz.	low-fat plain yogurt
½–1 teaspoon	chili powder
½ teaspoon	ground turmeric
1 tablespoon	Garlic Purée (see page 16)
1 tablespoon	Ginger Purée (see page 17)
½ teaspoon	salt or to taste
2 teaspoons	cumin seeds
2 tablespoons	chopped fresh cilantro

➔ Score both sides of the chicken pieces with a sharp knife and put them in a large bowl. Mix all the remaining ingredients, except the cumin seeds and cilantro, and rub this mixture into the chicken. Cover and leave to marinate for 3–4 hours or overnight in the refrigerator. Bring the chicken to room temperature before cooking it.

➔ Preheat the grill to high and line a grill pan (without the rack) with foil. Lightly brush the foil with oil and place the chicken pieces on it. Cook about 5 inches away from the heat source for 5 minutes.

✦ Turn the chicken pieces over and cook for an additional 5 minutes. Turn them again and reduce the heat to medium, then cook for 7–8 minutes more on each side.

✦ Meanwhile, preheat a small frying pan over medium heat. Add the cumin seeds and turn off the heat. Stir for 30–60 seconds or until the seeds release their aroma, then transfer them to a plate and cool slightly. Crush the seeds in a mortar with a pestle, or on a board using the back of a wooden spoon.

✦ Sprinkle the crushed cumin seeds on both sides of the chicken pieces and transfer them to a serving plate. Mix the cilantro with the cooking juices left on the foil, which should be rather like a paste. Spread the paste evenly over the chicken pieces and serve immediately.

Turkey in Orange Juice
Turkey Narangi

SERVINGS: 4
PREPARATION TIME: 20 minutes
COOKING TIME: 30–35 minutes
PER SERVING: Calories: 270; Fat: 7 g.; Saturated fat: 2 g.

This is a light and aromatic dish. As turkey breast meat is virtually fat-free, I have used a little oil here to help develop the flavors of the spices.

1 tablespoon	sunflower or canola oil
3	green cardamom pods, bruised
2 1-inch	pieces of cinnamon stick
2 teaspoons	Ginger Purée (see page 17)
2 teaspoons	Garlic Purée (see page 16)
1½ lbs.	turkey breast fillets, skinned and cut into 1-inch cubes
4½ oz.	low-fat plain yogurt
½ teaspoon	ground turmeric
¼–½ teaspoon	chili powder
1 tablespoon	Ground Roasted Coriander (see page 22)
1 teaspoon	Ground Roasted Cumin (see page 21)
8 oz.	Boiled Onion Purée (see page 18)
8 fl. oz.	freshly squeezed orange juice
1 teaspoon	salt or to taste
1 teaspoon	sugar
1–2	green chilies, seeded and cut into julienne strips
2 tablespoons	chopped fresh cilantro leaves

→ Heat the oil in a nonstick saucepan over low heat and add the cardamoms and cinnamon. Stir the spices for 15–20 seconds. Add the ginger and garlic purées, and fry for 2 minutes, stirring constantly.

→ Add the turkey and increase the heat to medium-high. Cook, stirring frequently, for 3–4 minutes or until the turkey is opaque.

→ Add the yogurt, turmeric, chili powder, ground coriander, and cumin. Cook for 3–4 minutes, stirring frequently, then increase the heat to high. Continue to cook, stirring frequently, for 5–6 minutes or until all the cooking juices have evaporated and the turkey begins to brown.

→ Add the onion purée and cook for 3–4 minutes, then strain the orange juice over the turkey. Add the salt and sugar and bring to a boil. Cover and simmer for 15–20 minutes or until the turkey is tender.

→ Add the chilies and cilantro. Cook for 1–2 minutes. Serve with rice and Spiced Sweet Potatoes (see page 200) or Cabbage with Ginger (see page 206).

Lamb Specialties

LAMB IS THE fattiest of meats and the fat it contains is saturated, therefore I have restricted the number of recipes in this section. The exact fat content depends on various factors, such as the age of the animal, the breed, and the cut of meat. The choice of cut is one area over which we can exercise discretion and it is important to select lean joints or cuts to minimize the fat. I have used leg meat in the majority of these recipes because it is the leanest cut. On a positive note, remember that, as well as being high in protein, lamb is a rich source of all the B vitamins, which maintain a healthy nervous system, as well as zinc, which is necessary for healthy growth, and iron, which prevents anemia.

Always trim off all visible fat before cutting or preparing the meat. Make sure you cook it slowly and gently, because high temperatures toughen meat. Despite the fact that there is no added fat in any of the recipes (which makes them lower in calories), they're all full of flavor.

In addition, all of these dishes freeze well. Thaw them in the refrigerator before reheating them slowly over gentle heat, adding a little warm water when necessary, if sauces begin to dry up.

Make sure the food is piping hot throughout before serving. To freeze dry dishes, such as the Marinated Leg of Lamb (see page 124) or Marinated Lamb Chops (see page 116), cook to the stage where basting is required, then cool and freeze the meat and the cooking juices separately. Thaw completely before finishing the cooking process just before serving.

Marinated Lamb Chops

TABAK MAAZ

SERVINGS: 4
PREPARATION TIME: 10–15 minutes
COOKING TIME: 35–40 minutes
PER SERVING: Calories: 175; Fat: 9 g.; Saturated fat: 4.5 g.

This is an adaptation of a much-loved recipe from the beautiful valley of Kashmir.

4	lamb chops (or 8 lamb cutlets)
10 fl. oz.	2% milk
2 teaspoons	Ginger Purée (see page 17)
½ teaspoon	freshly ground black pepper
pinch	saffron threads, pounded
1½ teaspoons	ground fennel seeds
1½ teaspoons	ground cumin
½ teaspoon	chili powder
4	cloves
2-inch piece	cinnamon stick, halved
4	green cardamom pods, bruised
1 teaspoon	salt or to taste
½ teaspoon	Garam Masala (see page 23)
1 tablespoon	chopped fresh mint (or ½ teaspoon dried mint)
1 teaspoon	finely chopped fresh cilantro leaves

→ Remove the rind and excess fat from the chops or cutlets. Bring a saucepan of water to a boil and add the chops. Bring back to a boil and cook for 2–3 minutes, then drain and rinse the meat.

→ Put the drained chops or cutlets into a nonstick saucepan, about 12 inches in diameter, and add the remaining ingredients, except the garam masala, mint, and fresh coriander. Place the saucepan over medium heat and stir until the milk begins to bubble. Reduce the heat to low, cover the pan, and cook for 30 minutes. Turn the chops over occasionally during cooking.

→ Remove the saucepan from the heat and lift out each chop or cutlet with a pair of tongs or a draining spoon and fork. Shake off the cooking liquid back into the pan and set the meat aside on a plate. Strain the cooking liquid and return it to the saucepan with the chops or cutlets.

→ Cook over medium heat for 3–4 minutes, turning the chops or cutlets frequently, until the stock has reduced to half its original quantity.

→ Add the garam masala, mint, and cilantro evenly over the chops and continue to cook for 4–5 minutes, turning as before, until the stock evaporates and the chops are browned. Serve with Chapatis (see page 188) and Almond Chutney (see page 225) or Fruit Raita (see page 218).

Stir-Fried Spiced Lamb

BHUNA GOSHT

SERVINGS: 4
PREPARATION TIME: 20–25 minutes
COOKING TIME: 1 hour 10 minutes
PER SERVING: Calories: 330; Fat: 16 g.; Saturated fat: 7.5 g.

Bhuna gosht is a much-loved dish in northern India. Its home is Delhi, the food-lover's paradise, where the exquisite Mogul cuisine dominates the scene. Bhuna, an important technique in Indian cooking, is similar to stir-frying. Spices are stir-fried in oil or ghee over a high heat, and a little water is added occasionally to ensure that the ingredients do not stick to the pan. In this version, I have fried the meat and the spices together in the fat naturally present in lamb and the result is delicious.

1½ lbs.	boneless shoulder of lamb, cut into 1-inch cubes, plus a few bones
2 oz.	low-fat plain yogurt
2	large onions, finely sliced
1 tablespoon	Ginger Purée (see page 17)
1 tablespoon	Garlic Purée (see page 16)
10–12	black peppercorns
4	brown cardamom pods, slit slightly on top
6	cloves
2 2-inch	pieces of cinnamon stick, halved
2	bay leaves
1–3	dried red chilies, chopped
1 tablespoon	Ground Roasted Cumin (see page 21)
2 teaspoon	Ground Roasted Coriander (see page 22)
½ teaspoon	ground turmeric
½–1 teaspoon	chili powder
1 teaspoon	salt or to taste
1 tablespoon	tomato purée

15 fl. oz.	warm water
½ teaspoon	Garam Masala (see page 23)
2 tablespoons	chopped fresh cilantro leaves
1–2	tomatoes, chopped

Serve with . . .

any type of bread or boiled basmati rice and a vegetable dish.

→ Place the lamb in a nonstick saucepan with the bones. Add the yogurt, onions, ginger and garlic purées, peppercorns, cardamoms, cloves, cinnamon stick, bay leaves, and dried red chilies. Place the pan over medium-high heat and stir until the contents begin to sizzle. Reduce the heat to medium, cover the pan, and cook for 30 minutes.

→ Remove the lid and increase the heat to high. Add the cumin, ground coriander, turmeric, chili powder, and salt. Cook, stirring constantly for 8–9 minutes. The spices will begin to stick to the pan halfway through—immediately add 2–3 tablespoons cold water and continue cooking, stirring, for 2–3 minutes. Repeat this process, adding cold water twice more.

→ Stir in the tomato purée and warm water until thoroughly mixed and reduce the heat to low, then cover the pan and cook for 20 minutes.

→ Remove the lid and cook for a few minutes to reduce the sauce, if necessary, until it is thick enough to coat the meat.

→ Stir in the garam masala, cilantro, and tomatoes. Cook for 1 minute, then remove and discard the bones.

Dry-Fried Lamb
Mangsher Jhalfrezi

Servings: 4
Preparation time: 15–20 minutes
Cooking time: 55–60 minutes
Per serving: Calories: 316; Fat: 15.5 g.; Saturated fat: 7.5 g.

Jhalfrezi is one of the most popular dishes from the rich and the varied cuisine of Bengal. In the Bengali language the word *jhal* means hot, but a jhalfrezi isn't meant to be chili hot; instead the heat comes from freshly ground black pepper and other spices such as cloves, cinnamon, and cardamom. The dish has a deliciously pungent thick sauce and is often garnished with fried onions, but for a lower-fat result you can add Browned Sliced Onions (see page 19).

1½ lbs.	boneless leg of lamb, cubed
1	large onion, finely chopped
1 tablespoon	Ginger Purée (see page 17)
1 tablespoon	Garlic Purée (see page 16)
1 teaspoon	freshly ground black pepper
6	cloves
1-inch	piece of cinnamon stick
4	green cardamom pods, bruised
1 teaspoon	paprika
½ teaspoon	ground turmeric
2 teaspoons	Ground Roasted Cumin (see page 21)
2 teaspoons	Ground Roasted Coriander (see page 22)
2½ oz.	low-fat plain yogurt
15 fl. oz.	warm water
1½ tablespoons	tomato purée
1 teaspoon	salt or to taste
1–2	green chilies, seeded and sliced lengthwise
2 tablespoons	chopped fresh cilantro leaves

✦ In a nonstick saucepan, about 12 inches in diameter, dry-fry half the meat over high heat for 3–4 minutes. Add the remaining meat and continue to cook, stirring frequently, until the meat begins to release its juices.

✦ Add the onion and cook for 5 minutes, stirring frequently. Stir in the ginger and garlic purées, and continue to cook for 8–9 minutes or until all the liquid evaporates. Reduce the heat to medium halfway through cooking.

✦ Add the pepper, cloves, cinnamon stick, cardamoms, paprika, turmeric, cumin, and ground coriander, and stir-fry for 1 minute, then add half the yogurt. Continue to stir-fry for an additional 1 minute. Add the remaining yogurt and cook for 30–40 seconds.

✦ Pour in the water, then stir in the tomato purée and salt. Bring to a boil, cover and reduce the heat to low, then cook for 30–35 minutes or until the lamb is tender.

✦ Remove the lid and cook over medium heat for 3–4 minutes or until the sauce has thickened. Stir in the chilies and cilantro leaves and cook for 1 minute. Serve with Chapatis (see page 188) and a raita.

Variation

You can use chicken instead of the lamb, but reduce the amount of water to 8 fl. oz. The cooking time is about 20 minutes for boneless chicken or 30 to 35 minutes for chicken on the bone.

Baked Kebabs

Dum ke Kabab

SERVINGS: 4
PREPARATION TIME: 10 minutes
COOKING TIME: 35 minutes
PER SERVING: Calories: 425; Fat: 23.5 g.; Saturated fat: 8.5 g.

This recipe is based on a traditional north Indian dish in which ground mutton is used. I have used lean ground lamb, although you could use ground chicken or turkey instead. It is excellent served with Fruit Raita (see page 218) and any bread.

10–12	blanched almonds, roughly chopped
2 tablespoons	channa dhal or yellow split peas
1 tablespoon	sunflower seeds
2–3	dried red chilies, chopped
2 tablespoons	white poppy seeds
1½ lbs.	lean ground lamb
1 tablespoon	Ginger Purée (see page 17)
1 tablespoon	Garlic Purée (see page 16)
½ teaspoon	ground turmeric
1 teaspoon	paprika
1 tablespoon	finely chopped fresh mint (or ½ teaspoon dried mint)
2 tablespoons	chopped fresh cilantro leaves
1 teaspoon	Garam Masala (see page 23)
1 teaspoon	salt or to taste

Garnish with . . .
2 eggs, hard-boiled and sliced; 1 red onion, halved and finely sliced; 1 large tomato, sliced; wedged of lime or lemon; and 1 green chili, seeded and cut into julienne strips.

➺ Preheat a small frying pan over medium heat. When hot, turn the heat down to low and add the almonds. Stir for 1 minute, then add the channa dhal, sunflower seeds, and chilies (in this order). Stir and roast for 1 minute, then add the poppy seeds. Roast for an additional 1 minute, stirring, then remove from the heat. Do not allow the poppy seeds to darken. Transfer the ingredients to a plate. Allow to cool, then grind them in a coffee or spice mill until fine. Do not worry if the almonds aren't finely ground.

→ Put the lamb in a large bowl and add the ground mixture along with all the remaining ingredients. Mix thoroughly and knead for 1–2 minutes. Cover and set aside for 30 minutes. Meanwhile, preheat the oven to 375°F.

→ Spread the spiced lamb in a 12 x 6-inch ovenproof dish. Using the back of a metal spoon, tidy up the edges by pushing them inwards to make a neat, oblong shape, then smooth the top. Bake for 30 minutes.

→ Allow to rest for 3–4 minutes, then cut into squares and transfer to a serving dish. Strain the cooking juices, brush a little over the kebabs, and discard the remainder. Serve surrounded with the garnishing ingredients.

COOK'S TIP: Roasted channa dhal and white poppy seeds add a distinctive flavor. You can get these from Indian stores, large supermarkets, and health food shops.

Marinated Leg of Lamb
RAAN

SERVINGS: 6
PREPARATION TIME: 30 minutes, plus marinating
COOKING TIME: 1 hour 40 minutes
PER SERVING: Calories: 490; Fat: 28 g.; Saturated fat: 11.5 g.

The method of cooking a *raan* (leg of lamb) was first invented by the Mongolian warrior Chengiz Khan (A.D. 1162–1227), when it was known as the Chengezi Raan. The lamb was flavored with a simple spice mix and roasted on a spit over a wood fire. Since then the recipe has been refined and different versions have been created, many elevated to such grand styles that they graced the tables of Emperors and Maharajas. My version has a fabulously opulent flavor despite being free from the usual ghee or butter.

6½ lbs.	leg of lamb
2½ fl. oz.	light malt vinegar
1½ teaspoons	salt or to taste
8 oz.	low-fat plain yogurt
1½ tablespoons	Ginger Purée (see page 17)
1½ tablespoons	Garlic Purée (see page 16)
2½ oz.	Browned Onion Purée (see page 20)
pinch	saffron threads, pounded
½ teaspoon	ground turmeric
1 teaspoon	black peppercorns
	seeds from 6 green cardamom pods
4	cloves
1	blade of mace
1½ tablespoons	white poppy seeds
1 tablespoon	sesame seeds
1 oz.	unroasted cashew nut pieces
1 oz.	raisins
5 fl. oz.	boiling water
1 tablespoon	flaked almonds, toasted, to garnish

+ Trim excess fat and any membrane from the lamb. Prick it all over with the point of a small sharp knife or a fork. Place the lamb in a large shallow dish and pour the vinegar over it, then sprinkle with the salt. Rub the salt well into the meat, then set it aside.

+ Mix the yogurt, ginger, garlic and onion purées, saffron, and turmeric. Grind the peppercorns, cardamom seeds, cloves, mace, poppy and sesame seeds to a fine powder in a coffee or spice mill and stir into the yogurt mixture.

+ Transfer the lamb to a large dish, discarding the vinegar, and rub the yogurt mixture all over the meat. Cover and chill for 24–36 hours. Bring the lamb to room temperature before cooking.

+ Preheat the oven to 425°F. Put the leg of lamb in a roasting tin and cover with foil, tenting the foil so that it doesn't touch the meat. Alternatively, use a covered roasting dish.

+ Cook for 20 minutes, then reduce the temperature to 375°F. Cook for an additional 35 minutes.

+ Meanwhile, soak the cashews and raisins in the boiling water for 15 minutes, then purée them in a blender with the water in which they were soaked. Baste the meat generously with the cooking juices, then spread with the puréed nut mixture. Cover and continue cooking for 30–35 minutes.

+ Uncover and baste the lamb, then cook for 8–10 minutes. Remove the meat from the oven, cover it loosely with foil and set it aside to rest for 15–20 minutes. To serve, cut the meat into chunky pieces and pour over any cooking juices left in the roasting dish. Garnish with the toasted almonds and serve. Spiced Chapatis (see page 190) or Vegetable Pilau (see page 186) and a raita are suitable accompaniments.

Lamb in Coconut Milk

Nariyal ka Gosht

SERVINGS: 4
PREPARATION TIME: 20 minutes, plus marinating
COOKING TIME: 1 hour 10 minutes
PER SERVING: Calories: 380; Fat: 24 g.; Saturated fat: 15 g.

This delectable dish originates from the southern coastal region where coconut palm is a major crop. Besides being used extensively in cooking, a thriving industry has developed around the non-food by-products of coconut.

The fat content of this recipe is quite high as it contains creamed coconut (the only recipe in the book to do so). Treat it as an occasional luxury.

2½ oz.	low-fat plain yogurt
1 tablespoon	Ginger Purée (see page 17)
1 tablespoon	Garlic Purée (see page 16)
1	large onion, finely chopped
½ teaspoon	ground turmeric
½–1 teaspoon	chili powder
1 teaspoon	paprika
1½ lbs.	boneless leg of lamb, cut into 1-inch cubes, plus 8 oz. bones
1½ tablespoons	Ground Roasted Coriander (see page 22)
1½ teaspoons	Ground Roasted Cumin (see page 21)
2 oz.	creamed coconut, grated, or desiccated coconut, ground in a coffee or spice mill until smooth
10 fl. oz.	warm water
1 teaspoon	salt or to taste
½ teaspoon	Garam Masala (see page 23)
2–3	green chilies, with the stalks intact
2–3 tablespoons	chopped fresh cilantro leaves
1 tablespoon	lime juice

→ Mix the yogurt, ginger and garlic purées, onion, turmeric, chili powder, and paprika in a large mixing bowl and add the meat. Mix thoroughly, cover the bowl, and leave to marinate for 2 hours or overnight in the refrigerator. Bring it to room temperature before cooking.

→ Put the marinated meat in a nonstick saucepan, about 12 inches in diameter, and place over high heat. Stir until the meat begins to sizzle. Reduce the heat to low, cover the pan and cook for 25–30 minutes, stirring occasionally. There should be very little liquid left at the end of the cooking time (2–3 tablespoons). If necessary, cook, uncovered, over medium heat to reduce the liquid.

→ Add the ground coriander and cumin, and cook over low heat for 3–4 minutes, stirring frequently. Stir in the coconut, warm water, and salt. Cover the pan and simmer for 20–25 minutes, stirring occasionally.

→ Add the garam masala, chilies, and cilantro. Cook, uncovered, for 1–2 minutes, then stir in the lime juice and remove from the heat. Remove the bones and serve with Cinnamon Rice (see page 175) and Fresh Vegetable Pickle (see page 228).

COOK'S TIP: If you have any prepared Aromatic Stock (see page 25), use it instead of the water in the above recipe and omit the bones.

COOK'S TIP: If you're unable to find creamed coconut, just replace it with desiccated coconut ground in a coffee grinder and moistened with boiling water before adding to the curry.

Lamb with Spinach
Palak Gosht

SERVINGS: 4
PREPARATION TIME: 20–25 minutes
COOKING TIME: 1 hour 10 minutes
PER SERVING: Calories: 325; Fat: 16 g.; Saturated fat: 7.5 g.

Lamb with spinach originated in Punjab, a state known for its rugged richness. The Punjabis are an energetic and fun-loving people with a particular flair for good food. Wheat and corn grow abundantly in the state (known as the granary of the nation) and Punjabis thrive on bread. Traditionally, this dish would be drenched in ghee (clarified butter), but this oil-free version has its own characteristic taste and aroma. Serve it with any bread in the true Punjabi style.

1½ lbs.	boneless shoulder or leg of lamb, cut into 1-inch cubes, plus a few bones
2 oz.	low-fat plain yogurt
1 tablespoon	Garlic Purée (see page 16)
1 tablespoon	Ginger Purée (see page 17)
1 tablespoon	ground coriander
1½ teaspoons	ground cumin
2 2-inch	pieces of cinnamon stick, halved
6	green cardamom pods, bruised
½ teaspoon	ground turmeric
½–1 teaspoon	chili powder
8 oz.	Boiled Onion Purée (see page 18)
1 tablespoon	tomato purée
1 teaspoon	salt or to taste
10 fl. oz.	warm water
8 oz.	fresh spinach, finely chopped, or frozen leaf spinach, thawed and drained
½ teaspoon	Garam Masala (see page 23)

Garnish

1	tomato, finely chopped
1 tablespoon	chopped fresh cilantro leaves

→ Put the meat into a nonstick saucepan and add the bones. Add the yogurt, garlic and ginger purées, ground coriander, cumin, cinnamon stick, cardamoms, turmeric, and chili powder. Place over medium-high heat and stir until the mixture begins to sizzle. Reduce the heat to low, cover and cook for 30–35 minutes, stirring occasionally. Remove the lid and increase the heat to high. Cook until all the liquid evaporates, stirring frequently.

→ Add the boiled onion purée, tomato purée, and salt. Continue to cook, stirring constantly, for an additional 3–4 minutes. Pour in the warm water and bring to a boil. Reduce the heat to low, cover the pan and cook for 20–25 minutes or until the meat is tender.

→ Add the spinach and stir until the leaves wilt. Cook, uncovered, over a medium heat for 3–4 minutes, stirring occasionally. Reduce the heat to low, cover the pan and cook for 5–7 minutes.

→ Finally, stir in the garam masala and cook for 1 minute. Transfer to a serving dish and garnish with the chopped tomato. Sprinkle with chopped cilantro and serve immediately.

Pork Main Meals

WE TEND TO think of pork as a fatty meat and, therefore, not suitable for healthy eating. In fact, with the exception of some cuts and many pork products (such as sausages and fatty bacon, for example), pork is one of the leanest meats available.

When I read about different types and cuts of meat to include in this book, I was surprised to discover that, not only is pork lower in fat than lamb or beef, but it is also only marginally fattier than chicken (with skin). Pork is a protein food that offers all the B vitamins, iron, and zinc. As long as all the visible fat is removed, pork fits in extremely well as part of a healthy diet.

In Indian cooking, because of various religious taboos and socioeconomic conditions, pork isn't a widely used meat. Besides Goa, on the west coast, and the warrior community of Coorg in South India, where people cook an excellent range of pork dishes, only the tribal people in the hilly terrains of the northeast cook pork extensively.

Spiced Ground Pork with Mushrooms

KHEEMA-KHUMB MASALA

SERVINGS: 4
PREPARATION TIME: 10 minutes, plus marinating
COOKING TIME: 22–25 minutes
PER SERVING: Calories: 200; Fat: 8.5 g.; Saturated fat: 2.9 g.

This easy recipe makes a quick mid-week meal. It is a dry dish for which dhal or a vegetable curry are ideal accompaniments. Serve either Chapatis (see page 188) or boiled basmati rice to complete the meal

1 lb.	lean ground pork
2 teaspoons	Ginger Purée (see page 17)
2 teaspoons	Garlic Purée (see page 16)
1/2 teaspoon	ground turmeric
1/2 teaspoon	chili powder
2 oz.	low-fat plain yogurt
1 teaspoon	Ground Roasted Cumin (see page 21)
2 teaspoons	Ground Roasted Coriander (see page 22)
8 oz.	Boiled Onion Purée (see page 18)
1 teaspoon	salt or to taste
8 oz.	button mushrooms, quartered
1 tablespoon	tomato purée
1/2 teaspoon	Garam Masala (see page 23)
1–2	green chilies, seeded and cut into julienne strips
2 tablespoons	finely chopped fresh cilantro

→ In a mixing bowl, combine the ground pork, ginger, and garlic purées, turmeric, chili powder, and yogurt. Mix thoroughly, cover, and set aside for 30 minutes.

→ Put the mixture in a nonstick sauté pan or frying pan, at least 10 inches in diameter. Cook over medium-high heat for 7–8 minutes, stirring regularly, until the mixture is dry.

→ Add the cumin and ground coriander. Continue to cook for 1 minute, then add the onion purée and salt, and cook for an additional 3–4 minutes, stirring regularly.

→ Mix in the mushrooms and tomato purée. Sprinkle 2–3 tablespoons water over the mixture and cover the pan. Reduce the heat to low and cook for 8–10 minutes, stirring once or twice to ensure that the contents do not stick to the bottom of the pan. If dry, add a little more water.

→ Stir in the garam masala, chilies, and cilantro. Cook for 1 minute, then serve immediately.

Goan Pork Curry
PORK BAFFADO

SERVINGS: 4
PREPARATION TIME: 15–20 minutes, plus marinating
COOKING TIME: 55–60 minutes
PER SERVING: Calories: 308; Fat: 12 g.; Saturated fat: 4.3 g.

Goa is probably the only state in India where pork and beef are sold and consumed as a matter of habit. Hindus, who do not eat beef, and Muslims, who do not eat pork, live in close harmony with Christians, and each group respects the others' choice of meat. The cuisine of Goa has a predominantly Portuguese influence.

1 lb.	boneless leg of pork
2 tablespoons	cider vinegar
2 teaspoons	Ginger Purée (see page 17)
2 teaspoons	Garlic Purée (see page 16)
½ teaspoon	ground turmeric
2 teaspoons	paprika
8½ fl. oz.	medium-sweet cider
1-inch	piece of cinnamon stick, broken up
6	cloves
½ teaspoon	black peppercorns
½ teaspoon	black mustard seeds
1½ teaspoons	cumin seeds
1 teaspoon	salt or to taste
1 teaspoon	soft brown sugar
9 oz.	Boiled Onion Purée (see page 18)
1 tablespoon	tomato purée
11 fl. oz.	warm water
2–4	green chilies, seeded and cut into julienne strips

FROM THE TOP:
Fresh Tomato Chutney (page 227),
Fish Tikka (page 30),
Steamed Pork Balls (page 43),
and Indian Cheese Kebabs (page 40)

Fruit Curry (page 216)
and Saffron Rice (page 176)

Baked Kebabs (page 122)
and Fruit Raita (page 218)

Lentils with Kidney Beans (page 153)
Tandoori Bread (page 192)

Chicken in Apricot Juice (page 84),
Carrots and Green Beans with Poppy Seeds (page 204),
and Spiced Chapatis (page 190)

Spiced Pork Chops (page 138)
with Eggplant Pilau (page 184)
and Pineapple Raita (page 220)

Jumbo Shrimp with Baby Zucchini (page 59)
and Cumin-Coriander Rice (page 174)

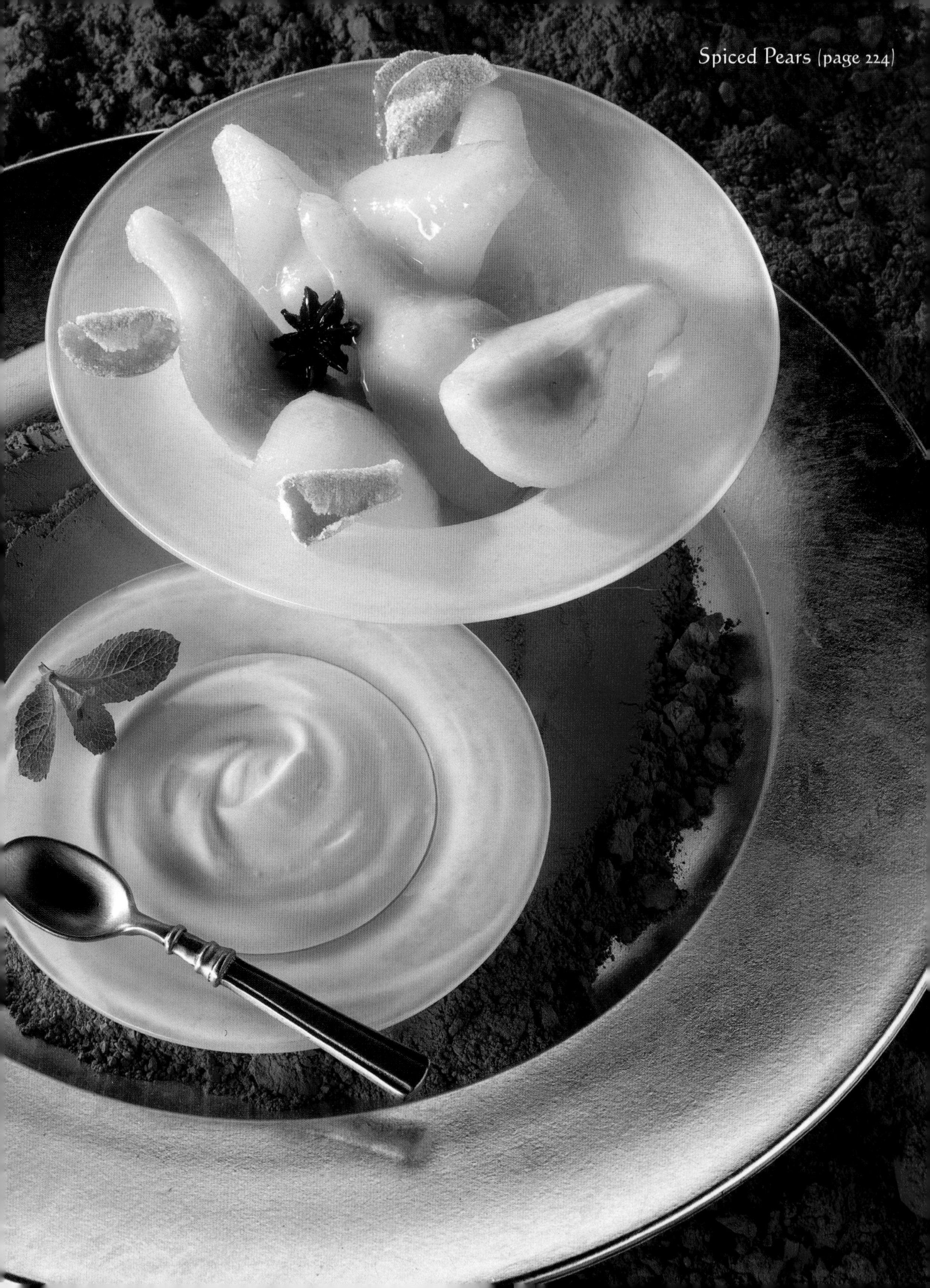

Spiced Pears (page 224)

→ Remove the rind and any visible fat from the pork. Cut the lean meat into 1-inch cubes and put into a large mixing bowl.

→ Mix the vinegar, ginger and garlic purées, turmeric, and paprika, and pour over the meat. Stir until the meat is fully coated, then cover the bowl and set aside for 1–2 hours or overnight in the refrigerator. Bring it to room temperature before cooking.

→ Put the marinated meat in a nonstick saucepan, about 12 inches in diameter, and place over medium-high heat. Stir for 4–5 minutes or until the pork turns opaque.

→ Pour in the cider and bring to simmering point. Cover the pan and reduce the heat to medium-low, then cook for 35–40 minutes or until the liquid resembles a thin batter.

→ Meanwhile, preheat a small pan over medium heat. When hot, reduce the heat to low and add the whole spices. Roast the spices gently for 30–60 seconds, stirring all the time, until they release their aroma, then transfer them to a plate and cool for a few minutes.

→ Grind the spices finely in a coffee or spice mill and add to the meat with the salt and sugar. Increase the heat slightly and cook until all the liquid has evaporated, stirring frequently.

→ Add the onion purée and continue to cook for an additional 3–4 minutes, then stir in the tomato purée and water. Reduce the heat to low, cover the pan, and simmer gently for 8–10 minutes or until the sauce has thickened.

→ Add the chilies and simmer for an additional 1–2 minutes. Serve with boiled basmati rice or Cinnamon Rice (see page 175) and Cucumber and Peanut Salad (see page 231).

Pork Vindaloo
SHIKAR VINDALOO

SERVINGS: 4
PREPARATION TIME: 20 minutes, plus marinating
COOKING TIME: 55–60 minutes
PER SERVING: Calories: 306; Fat: 12.5 g.; Saturated fat: 4.4 g.

Although vindaloo is probably the most famous export from Goa, its origins are Portuguese. Portuguese traders landed on the west coast of India in the 16th century in search of silks, spices, and ivory, and history has it that they carried pork, preserved in vinegar, garlic, and black pepper, to last their voyage. The word *vin* comes from vinegar and *aloo* is derived from *alho,* meaning garlic in Portuguese. The recipe has been changed to a great extent by Indian influence and this is a low-fat version.

1½ lbs.	boneless leg of pork
4	green cardamom pods
4	cloves
1-inch	piece of cinnamon stick, broken
½ teaspoon	black mustard seeds
¼ teaspoon	fenugreek seeds
½ teaspoon	black peppercorns
3–8	dried red chilies, coarsely chopped
2 teaspoons	Ginger Purée (see page 17)
2 teaspoons	Garlic Purée (see page 16)
2 tablespoons	cider vinegar
8½ fl. oz.	medium-sweet cider
2 teaspoons	paprika
1¼ teaspoons	salt or to taste
9 oz.	Boiled Onion Purée (see page 18)
11 fl. oz.	warm water
½ teaspoon	tamarind concentrate or 1 tablespoon tamarind pulp
1 teaspoon	soft brown sugar

Serve with . . .

boiled basmati rice and a raita or a dry spiced vegetable dish.

→ Remove the rind from the pork and trim off any visible fat. Cut the lean meat into 1-inch cubes and put in a large bowl.

→ Preheat a small pan over medium heat. When hot, reduce the heat to low and add all the whole spices and dried red chilies. Roast the spices gently for 30–60 seconds, stirring all the time, until they release their aroma. Transfer the spices to a plate and leave to cool for 5 minutes, then grind them finely in a coffee or spice mill.

→ Thoroughly mix the ginger and garlic purées, vinegar, and the ground roasted spices, then add to the meat. Stir until the meat is fully coated, cover, and leave to marinate for 2–3 hours or overnight in the refrigerator. Bring the meat to room temperature before cooking.

→ Put the meat and its marinade in a nonstick saucepan, about 12 inches in diameter, and place over medium-high heat. Stir until the pork turns opaque, then pour in the cider. Bring just to a boil, cover the pan and cook over medium-low heat for 35–40 minutes or until the liquid is reduced to the consistency of a thin batter.

→ Uncover the pan and increase the heat slightly. Continue to cook for an additional 3–4 minutes or until the moisture has evaporated completely.

→ Add the paprika and salt, cook for 2–3 minutes stirring constantly, then stir in the onion purée. Continue to cook for 4–5 minutes, stirring regularly.

→ Pour in the water and stir in the tamarind and sugar. Cover and simmer gently for 10–12 minutes, stirring occasionally.

Variation

Use leg of lamb instead of pork.

Spiced Pork Chops
Masala Chaamp

SERVINGS: 4
PREPARATION TIME: 15–20 minutes, plus marinating
COOKING TIME: 15 minutes
PER SERVING: Calories: 220; Fat: 10.5 g.; Saturated fat: 4.7 g.

Marinated pork chops are delicious when pan-roasted or grilled. As well as yogurt, I have used a little pineapple in the marinade because the enzyme it contains is an excellent tenderizing agent. Serve with Eggplant Pilau (see page 184) and Pineapple Raita (see page 220).

4	pork chops, boned shoulder or leg steaks

Marinade

3 oz.	low-fat plain yogurt
3 oz.	low-fat sour cream
3 oz.	fresh pineapple, coarsely chopped
2–3 tablespoons	chopped onions
2 teaspoons	Ginger Purée (see page 17)
2 teaspoons	Garlic Purée (see page 16)
½ teaspoon	ground turmeric
½–1 teaspoon	chili powder
1 teaspoon	salt or to taste
½ teaspoon	sugar

Basting sauce

1 teaspoon	Ground Roasted Cumin (see page 21)
¼ teaspoon	chili powder (optional)
1 teaspoon	tomato ketchup
1 tablespoon	finely chopped fresh cilantro
1 teaspoon	sugar
pinch	salt

→ Remove any rind and excess fat from the chops. Prick the chops all over with a fork to allow flavors to penetrate, then put them in a shallow dish.

→ Put all the ingredients for the marinade in a blender or food processor and blend or process until well mixed. Pour this marinade over the chops and mix thoroughly. Cover and refrigerate for 4–6 hours or overnight. Bring the chops to room temperature before cooking.

→ Preheat the grill to high for 8–10 minutes. Line the grill pan (without the rack) with aluminum foil. Lightly brush the foil with oil.

→ Using a pair of tongs, lift each chop out of the dish and shake off any excess marinade back into the dish. Place the chops on the prepared grill pan and cook, 3 inches away from the heat source, for 4–5 minutes or until the chops are slightly charred. Turn them over and cook for an additional 3–4 minutes or until charred as before.

→ Mix all the ingredients for the basting sauce with the remaining marinade and add 2 tablespoons water, then brush half the mixture over the chops. Cook for 2–3 minutes, turn the chops over, and repeat with the remaining basting sauce.

→ Transfer the chops to a warmed serving plate and strain any remaining cooking sauce over them. Serve immediately.

Meatball Curry

KOFTA KARI

SERVINGS: 4
PREPARATION TIME: 20–25 minutes
COOKING TIME: 40–45 minutes
PER SERVING: Calories: 200; Fat: 8 g.; Saturated fat: 2.8 g.

Lean pork meatballs, simmered in a rich tomato sauce, are a delicious alternative to the traditional lamb or mutton version. Buy good-quality lean ground pork from supermarkets or make it yourself at home by removing all visible fat and chopping the meat into small pieces, then processing in the food processor until finely ground.

Meatballs

1 lb.	lean ground pork
2 teaspoons	Ginger Purée (see page 17)
1 teaspoon	Garlic Purée (see page 16)
1–2	green chilies, seeded and chopped
1	small onion, coarsely chopped
½ oz.	fresh cilantro leaves and stalks
1 teaspoon	salt or to taste
1 teaspoon	Garam Masala (see page 23)

Tomato sauce

14 oz.	canned chopped tomatoes or 1 lb. fresh tomatoes, skinned and chopped
1–2	green chilies, seeded and chopped
1 teaspoon	Garlic Purée (see page 16)
1 teaspoon	Ginger Purée (see page 17)
2-inch	piece of cinnamon stick, halved
6	cloves
1 teaspoon	salt or to taste

1½ teaspoons	sugar
½ teaspoon	Ground Roasted Cumin (see page 21)
2 tablespoons	chopped fresh cilantro leaves

Serve with . . .

any type of bread or boiled basmati rice, and a raita or salad.

→ Line a grill pan (without the rack) with aluminum foil and brush lightly with oil.

→ Put all the ingredients for the meatballs in a food processor and blend until smooth. Divide into 16 golf-ball-sized portions and shape into neat rounds by rotating and pressing gently between your palms so that the mixture is quite compact. Place the meatballs in a single layer on the prepared pan.

→ Preheat the grill to high. Grill the meatballs 3 inches below the heat source for 4–5 minutes or until browned. Turn the meatballs and cook for 3–4 minutes or until browned. Remove and set aside.

→ Put all the ingredients for the sauce (except the ground cumin and cilantro) in a saucepan and add 2½ fl. oz. water. Bring to simmering point, cover and cook for 15 minutes.

→ Cool the sauce slightly, remove the whole spices and either purée in a blender or press through a sieve.

→ Put the cooked meatballs in a nonstick saucepan and pour the sauce over. Cover and cook over low heat for 12–15 minutes, stirring occasionally.

→ Stir in the ground cumin and fresh cilantro until thoroughly mixed.

Spiced Pork Burgers
MASALA SHIKAR KI TIKKI

SERVINGS: 4
PREPARATION TIME: 10–15 minutes
COOKING TIME: 10–12 minutes
PER SERVING: Calories: 200; Fat: 8.5 g.; Saturated fat: 3 g.

I had to include this recipe for my children, and all other children, who have a taste for spicy food. The meat is bound with bread soaked in milk. The lactic acid in the milk tenderizes the meat, giving a melt-in-your-mouth result. Lean ground lamb or chicken can be used instead of pork. I serve these with French fries made by coating the cut potatoes with a little olive oil and cooking them in a hot oven.

1	large slice of white bread, crusts removed
2½ fl. oz.	2% milk
1 lb.	lean ground pork
1 teaspoon	Ginger Purée (see page 17)
1 teaspoon	Garlic Purée (see page 16)
1 oz.	fresh cilantro leaves and stalks
1 teaspoon	Garam Masala (see page 23)
1 teaspoon	salt or to taste
2 tablespoons	finely chopped scallions

Basting sauce

½ teaspoon	ground cumin
1 tablespoon	tomato ketchup

Serve with . . .
   4 burger buns and 4 slices of reduced-fat cheese (optional).

- → Soak the bread in the milk for 5 minutes, then squeeze out the milk. Put the bread in a food processor with the remaining ingredients except the scallions. Blend until smooth, then transfer the mixture to a bowl and add the scallions. Mix well.
- → Divide the mixture into quarters and shape each portion into a burger.
- → Preheat the grill to high and blend the ingredients for the basting sauce together in a small bowl, adding 2 fl. oz. water.
- → Cook the burgers 5 inches below the heat source for 4–5 minutes. Brush with basting sauce and cook for an additional 2–3 minutes. Turn the burgers and brush with the remaining sauce. Cook for 3–4 minutes.
- → Meanwhile, split and warm the buns and spread them with more tomato ketchup, if liked. Place a burger on the bottom half of each bun and top with cheese (if using). Place under the grill until the cheese begins to melt. Place the tops of the buns on the burgers and serve immediately.

Vegetarian Main Meals

ALTHOUGH I'M NOT a strict vegetarian, I have been brought up to believe that a vegetarian diet maintains a healthy mind as well as a healthy body. In recent years, the trend toward eating wholesome vegetarian food has gathered momentum, with an accusing finger pointed squarely at red meat, animal fat, and sweets. Although the tendency toward eating vegetarian meals is now more common in the West, many people are still concerned about whether a solely vegetarian diet provides the essential nutrients required by the body.

In this section, I have grouped the dishes containing vegetarian protein. Legumes are the cheapest alternative to meat and combining them with vegetables and a staple, such as rice or bread, is the simple principle of a healthy and balanced vegetarian diet. As well as providing protein, they're also low in fat and high in fiber, and provide important vitamins and minerals.

India grows an amazing array of beans and lentils, which are used imaginatively to make a variety of dishes, from those for simple, everyday meals to elaborate and exotic creations. A lentil dish takes hardly any effort because most of the preparation time is spent simmering the ingredients, during which time other dishes can be prepared for the meal.

There are literally thousands of different ways in which lentils are used in everyday Indian cooking. Whole lentils add a distinctive, nutty flavor to vegetable dishes. They can be soaked and ground, then mixed to a batter for making pancakes. Roasted and ground, they're used to make chutneys or to thicken sauces.

The other source of protein in the Indian vegetarian diet is paneer, the homemade Indian cheese, which is now produced on a commercial scale. You may find paneer in some supermarkets, and it is of course available in Indian stores.

Please don't think that I am trying to convert you to a vegetarian diet—I am merely attempting to convince you to sample the simple joys of cooking and eating meals without fish, poultry, or meat.

Butter Beans with Spinach

PAVTA-PALAK

SERVINGS: 4
PREPARATION TIME: 20 minutes
COOKING TIME: 35 minutes
PER SERVING: Calories: 170; Fat: 7 g.; Saturated fat: 3 g.

Butter beans have a delicious, nutty taste and a smooth, buttery texture. Dried beans have to be soaked for several hours and boiled until tender. Canned beans, if well rinsed, work very well and save time. Cooked with spinach, butter beans taste and look splendid.

1 tablespoon	sunflower or canola oil
1-inch	piece of cinnamon stick
1	onion, finely chopped
1 teaspoon	Ginger Purée (see page 17)
1–2	green chilies, seeded and finely chopped
½ teaspoon	ground turmeric
½ teaspoon	chili powder
½ teaspoon	Ground Roasted Cumin (see page 21)
1 teaspoon	Ground Roasted Coriander (see page 22)
8 oz. tomatoes,	skinned and chopped, or canned chopped tomatoes with their juice
1 teaspoon	salt or to taste
9 oz.	spinach, finely chopped, or frozen leaf spinach
14 oz.	canned butter beans, drained and well rinsed
2½ fl. oz.	fat-free half-and-half
2½ fl. oz.	warm water

→ In a nonstick saucepan, heat the oil over low heat, then add the cinnamon stick and let it sizzle for 20–25 seconds. Add the onion, ginger purée, and green chilies. Increase the heat slightly and fry for 5–6 minutes, stirring regularly to ensure even cooking.

→ Stir in the turmeric, chili powder, cumin, and coriander. Cook for 30 seconds before adding the tomatoes. Continue to cook for 4–5 minutes, stirring frequently.

→ Add the salt and spinach, and stir until the spinach wilts. Cover the pan and reduce the heat to low, then cook for 10 minutes.

→ Add the butter beans, half and half, and water. Re-cover and cook for an additional 10 minutes. Serve with any bread or Cumin-Coriander Rice (see page 174).

Chickpeas in Tomato Sauce
Tamatar ka Rasewala Choley

SERVINGS: 4
PREPARATION TIME: 15 minutes
COOKING TIME: 30–35 minutes
PER SERVING: Calories: 300; Fat: 11 g.; Saturated fat: 1.3 g.

*C*hickpeas have a firm texture and satisfying, nutty flavor. They're delicious in this spicy tomato sauce, especially when served with fresh Indian bread and a refreshing raita.

2 tablespoons	sunflower or canola oil
2 1-inch	pieces of cinnamon stick
6	green cardamom pods, bruised
6	cloves
1	large onion, finely chopped
1–2	green chilies, seeded and chopped
2 teaspoons	Ginger Purée (see page 17)
1/2 teaspoon	ground turmeric
1/4–1/2 teaspoon	chili powder
8 oz.	canned chopped tomatoes, with their juice
2 14-oz.	cans chickpeas, drained and well rinsed
1 1/2 teaspoons	salt or to taste
10 fl. oz.	warm water
1 teaspoon	Ground Roasted Cumin (see page 21)
1 tablespoon	chopped fresh cilantro leaves
1 tablespoon	chopped fresh mint (or 1/2 teaspoon dried mint)

Serve with . . .

any type of bread and a raita.

→ Heat the oil in a nonstick saucepan, about 7 inches in diameter, over low heat and add the cinnamon, cardamom and cloves. Let the spices sizzle gently for 20–25 seconds.

→ Add the onion, chilies, and ginger purée. Increase the heat slightly and cook, stirring regularly, for 8–10 minutes or until the onion begins to brown.

→ Stir in the turmeric, chili powder, and tomatoes. Cook for an additional 4–5 minutes, stirring frequently.

→ Add the chickpeas, salt, and water. Bring to a boil, reduce the heat to low and cover the pan, then simmer for 12–15 minutes.

→ Stir in the cumin, chopped cilantro, and mint. Simmer for 1–2 minutes.

Variation:

Use black-eyed peas instead of the chickpeas.

Chickpeas with Indian Cheese

CHOLEY-PANEER

SERVINGS: 4
PREPARATION TIME: 20 minutes
COOKING TIME: 25 minutes
PER SERVING: Calories: 244; Fat: 9.7 g.; Saturated fat: 1.6 g.

*P*aneer is used all over India in both sweet and savory dishes. In this dish, halloumi cheese (from Cyprus) can be used instead, but reduce the quantity of salt by half, as halloumi is salted.

8 oz.	paneer, cut into 2-inch cubes
2 tablespoons	sunflower or canola oil
1	small onion, finely chopped
2 teaspoons	Ginger Purée (see page 17)
2 teaspoons	Garlic Purée (see page 16)
1–2	green chilies, seeded and chopped
1¼ teaspoons	salt or to taste
½ teaspoon	ground turmeric
1 teaspoon	Ground Roasted Cumin (see page 21)
¼–½ teaspoon	chili powder
4½ oz.	Boiled Onion Purée (see page 18)
8 oz.	tomatoes, skinned and chopped, or canned chopped tomatoes with their juice
14 oz.	canned chickpeas, drained and well rinsed
4½ oz.	spinach, coarsely chopped, or frozen leaf spinach

- Bring a saucepan of water to a boil and add the paneer. Bring back to a boil and boil for 1 minute, then drain and set aside. This prepares the paneer to absorb all the flavors.
- Heat the oil over medium heat in a sauté pan, about 12 inches in diameter, and add the onion, ginger and garlic purées, and green chili. Fry for 2–3 minutes, then add the salt. The salt helps to draw out the onion juices, so that they cook longer without burning. Reduce the heat slightly and continue to cook for 5–7 minutes or until the onions are soft.
- Add the turmeric, cumin and chili powder. Cook for 1 minute, then add the onion purée. Cook for an additional 2–3 minutes.
- Increase the heat to medium and add the tomatoes. Cook for 2 minutes, then add the chickpeas. Cook for 4–5 minutes, stirring regularly.
- Finally, add the paneer and spinach, and cook for 5–6 minutes, stirring. Serve with Puffed Grilled Bread (see page 194), Chapatis (see page 188) or Cinnamon Rice (see page 175) and a raita.

Lentils with Kidney Beans
DHAL MAHARANI

SERVINGS: 4–6
PREPARATION TIME: 10 minutes
COOKING TIME: 50 minutes
PER SERVING: Calories: 364; Fat: 13 g.; Saturated fat: 5 g.

A classic dish from the state of Punjab, where whole urad dhal (black grams) are cooked with kidney beans. I find channa dhal or yellow split peas more visually appealing than urad dhal, as well as being easily accessible.

6 oz.	channa dhal (yellow split peas)
1 tablespoon	grated fresh ginger
2	green chilies, seeded and chopped
15 oz.	canned red kidney beans, drained and well rinsed
1 teaspoon	salt or to taste
4 fl. oz.	fat-free half-and-half
2 tablespoons	sunflower or vegetable oil
1	small onion, finely chopped
1/2 teaspoon	ground turmeric
1 teaspoon	Garam Masala (see page 23)
4 1/2 oz.	ripe tomatoes, chopped
2 tablespoons	chopped fresh cilantro leaves

Serve with . . .
Any type of bread or rice.

→ Wash the dhal or split peas thoroughly and put them in a heavy saucepan with half the ginger and half the chilies. Pour in 2¼ cups water. Bring to a boil, then reduce the heat to low and simmer, uncovered, for 30 minutes or until tender. Mash some of the cooked dhal with a wooden spoon, pressing it against the side of the pan and mixing well to achieve a thick texture.

→ Add the kidney beans, salt, and half-and-half. Simmer for 10 minutes.

→ Meanwhile, in a small saucepan, heat the oil over medium heat and fry the onion and remaining ginger and chilies for 6–7 minutes or until the onion is lightly browned.

→ Stir in the turmeric and garam masala and cook for 1 minute, then add the tomatoes and cilantro. Cook for an additional 1 minute. Reserve 1 tablespoon of this mixture and stir the remainder into the peas and beans. Garnish with the reserved onion and tomato mixture.

Steamed Semolina Cakes with Spicy Lentils
IDLI-SAMBAR

SERVINGS: 4–5; makes 18 idlis
PREPARATION TIME: 20 minutes, plus standing time
COOKING TIME: 45–50 minutes
PER SERVING: Calories: 261; Fat: 4.9 g.; Saturated fat: 0.8 g.
Each idli provides 18 calories; 0.8 g. fat (0.14 g. saturated fat). When served to 4,
each portion of sambar provides 180 calories; 1.3 g. fat (0.16 g. saturated fat).

*H*ot, soft, and fluffy steamed cakes (idlis) served with spiced lentils is the signature dish of Tamil Nadu in southern India. Steamed cakes can be made with a combination of rice and lentils, which are soaked and ground, then left to ferment before steaming, but this recipe uses semolina, which is easier and quicker. Idli-Sambar makes a balanced vegetarian meal.

Idlis

10 oz.	semolina
1 teaspoon	baking powder
½ teaspoon	bicarbonate of soda
½ teaspoon	crushed dried chilies
½ oz.	unroasted cashew nuts, chopped
1 tablespoon	finely chopped fresh cilantro leaves
½ teaspoon	salt or to taste
8 oz.	low-fat plain yogurt
15 fl. oz.	soda water

Sambar

8 oz.	toor dhal (see page 12)
½ teaspoon	ground turmeric
1	carrot, diced

4½ oz.	green beans, fresh or frozen, cut into 1-inch pieces
1½ teaspoons	salt or to taste
1 tablespoon	coriander seeds
1 teaspoon	cumin seeds
1–4	dried red chilies, broken up
½ teaspoon	black peppercorns
½ teaspoon	black mustard seeds
2 tablespoons	tamarind juice or ½ teaspoon tamarind concentrate
2 tablespoons	finely chopped fresh cilantro leaves and stalks

✢ Prepare the mixture for the idlis. In a mixing bowl, mix all the dry ingredients. Beat the yogurt until smooth, then stir it into the semolina mixture.

✢ Gradually add the soda water and mix until you have a thick paste, slightly softer than the consistency of a dropping cake mixture. If the mixture has any lumps, whisk it with a wire whisk. Cover the bowl and set aside for 30 minutes.

✢ Meanwhile, put the dhal in a saucepan and add the turmeric. Pour in 4 cups water. Bring to a boil, then reduce the heat to medium and cook for 3–4 minutes or until all the foam subsides. Reduce the heat to low, cover the pan, and cook for 20 minutes.

✢ Add the carrot, green beans, and salt to the dhal, re-cover, and continue to cook for an additional 10–15 minutes or until the vegetables are tender.

✢ Lightly brush the cups from an egg poacher with oil and prepare a steamer over a saucepan of boiling water for cooking the idlis. Place 1½ tablespoons idli mixture into each cup and steam them for 10 minutes. When cooked, remove and keep hot until all the mixture is cooked.

✢ While the idlis are steaming, preheat a small pan over medium heat. Add the coriander seeds and cumin seeds, dried red chilies, peppercorns, and mustard seeds, and reduce the heat to low. Stir and roast the spices for 30–60 seconds or until they begin to release their aroma. Transfer the spices to a plate and cool slightly, then grind to a fine powder in a coffee or spice mill.

✢ Add the ground roasted spices to the lentils followed by the tamarind. If you are using tamarind concentrate, stir until it is dissolved completely. Add the cilantro, remove from the heat, and serve with the steamed cakes (idlis).

COOK'S TIP: Traditionally, steel idli molds are used to cook the cakes, and Indian women cook them in a pressure cooker. The cups from an egg poacher work just as well and a steamer will do the job instead of a pressure cooker. You can serve the idlis as a snack with a chutney, such as Almond Chutney (see page 225), instead of the sambar. The sambar can be served with boiled rice instead of the idlis.

Spiced Mixed Lentils
Mila hua Masala Dhal

SERVINGS: 5
PREPARATION TIME: 15 minutes
COOKING TIME: 35 minutes
PER SERVING: Calories: 219; Fat: 6.3 g.; Saturated fat: 0.8 g.

*A*s a rule, no Indian meal is complete without a lentil dish—to the vast majority of vegetarians it is a very satisfying and wholesome main dish, and meat-eaters enjoy lentils as a side dish. Here, I have combined three types of lentils, but you can vary the combination or cook just one of them.

2½ oz.	red lentils
2½ oz.	green lentils
2½ oz.	skinless split mung beans (moong dhal)
2 tablespoons	sunflower or canola oil
½ teaspoon	black mustard seeds
½ teaspoon	cumin seeds
1-inch	cube of fresh ginger, cut into julienne strips
1–2	green chilies, seeded and cut into julienne strips
1–2	red chilies, seeded and cut into julienne strips
1 teaspoon	ground turmeric
1½ pints	hot water
1 teaspoon	salt or to taste
1 teaspoon	Ground Roasted Cumin (see page 21)
2 tablespoons	finely chopped fresh cilantro leaves

- ✦ Wash the three types of lentils together and leave to drain in a colander.
- ✦ Heat the oil over low heat in a nonstick saucepan, about 7 inches in diameter. When hot, add the mustard seeds. As soon as they pop, add the cumin seeds, followed by the ginger.
- ✦ Reserve a little of both types of chilies and add the remainder to the pan, then fry gently for 1–2 minutes.
- ✦ Add the turmeric and the lentils. Increase the heat slightly and fry for 4–5 minutes, stirring regularly, then pour in the water. Bring to a boil, reduce the heat to low, cover the pan and simmer for 25–30 minutes.
- ✦ Stir in the salt and cumin, and simmer for 1 minute.
- ✦ Stir in the cilantro and remove from the heat. Serve garnished with the reserved chilies. Offer Tandoori Bread (see page 192) and a raita as accompaniments; Cumin-Coriander Rice (see page 174), a raita, or a vegetable dish are also excellent with the lentils.

Pancakes with Spicy Potato Filling

MASALA DOSA

SERVINGS: 8
PREPARATION TIME: 10–15 minutes
COOKING TIME: 30–35 minutes
PER SERVING: Calories: 75; Fat: 2.6 g.; Saturated fat: 1.2 g.

Tamil Nadu in Southern India is the home of dosas, which are crispy pancakes filled with spiced potatoes and served with a chutney. The pancakes are traditionally made by grinding a mixture of rice and lentils together, then the mixture is fermented for 6–12 hours before cooking. This is my instant version, which is quite delicious.

Pancakes

4½ oz.	semolina
4½ oz.	ground rice
2½ oz.	plain flour
½ teaspoon	salt or to taste
5½ oz.	low-fat plain yogurt

Filling

1 tablespoon	desiccated coconut
2–4	dried red chilies, broken up
1 teaspoon	Ground Roasted Cumin (see page 21)
1 teaspoon	Ground Roasted Coriander (see page 22)
1 teaspoon	salt or to taste
2 teaspoons	lemon juice
1 tablespoon	sunflower or canola oil
½ teaspoon	black mustard seeds
½ teaspoon	ground turmeric

| 1¼ lbs. | new potatoes, boiled and cut into bite-sized pieces |
| 2 tablespoons | chopped fresh cilantro leaves |

→ First prepare the filling. Grind the coconut and chilies to a powder in a coffee or spice mill. Transfer the mixture to a small bowl and add the cumin, ground coriander, salt, lemon juice, and 2 fl. oz. water. Mix and set aside.

→ Heat the oil in a nonstick saucepan over low heat. Add the mustard seeds, then as soon as they start crackling, stir in the turmeric.

→ Add the potatoes and the coconut mixture. Stir until the potatoes are heated through and the liquid is completely absorbed. Stir in the chopped cilantro, then keep the filling hot over very low heat while you make the pancakes.

→ In a large mixing bowl mix the semolina, ground rice, flour, and salt. Mix the yogurt with 13½ fl. oz. water, then gradually add to the semolina mixture, whisking well with a wire whisk. Alternatively, put all the ingredients in a blender or food processor and blend until smooth.

→ Heat a large, heavy griddle or nonstick frying pan, at least 9 inches in diameter, over medium heat and brush the surface lightly with oil. Wait until the surface of the pan is really hot, then pour about 4½ fl. oz. batter from a measuring jug, spreading it quickly and evenly on the pan. Allow the mixture to cook and set for 2 minutes.

→ Sprinkle 1 tablespoon water around the edges, wait for 15–20 seconds, then turn the dosa over with a thin spatula. Cook for an additional 2–3 minutes or until brown patches show through underneath.

→ Place a little of the spiced potato mixture on top and roll it up. Keep hot until the remainder of the batter is cooked. Serve immediately, with Almond Chutney (see page 225).

COOK'S TIP: To keep the filled dosas hot, place them in a single layer in an ovenproof dish, cover with foil and place in a warm oven or hot grill compartment (with the heat source turned off). The filling and chutney can be made in advance and kept chilled until required. Reheat the filling gently in a nonstick pan or in the microwave.

Vegetable Korma

SUBZI KORMA

SERVINGS: 4
PREPARATION TIME: 30 minutes, plus soaking
COOKING TIME: 15 minutes
PER SERVING: Calories: 251; Fat: 13.4 g.; Saturated fat: 2.5 g.

Originating from royal kitchens, korma is a dish associated with affluence. Traditionally meat-based, various vegetarian kormas are made these days. This healthy eating version is based on the principles of a traditional northern korma, but, instead of using cream and/or dried whole milk, I have enriched the sauce with 2% milk and puréed cashew nuts. Sunflower seeds are also used to make up for the minimal use of cashews.

10 fl. oz.	reduced-fat milk
1 oz.	unroasted cashew nut pieces
½ oz.	sunflower seeds
8 oz.	carrots, cut diagonally into ⅛-inch slices
4½ oz.	baby corn cobs
2 teaspoons	lemon juice
4½ oz.	green beans, cut into 2-inch pieces
12 oz.	cauliflower, divided into 1-inch florets
2 tablespoons	sunflower or canola oil
½ teaspoon	caraway seeds
1-inch	piece of cinnamon stick
4	green cardamom pods, bruised
1	small onion, finely chopped
1 teaspoon	Ginger Purée (see page 17)
1 teaspoon	Garlic Purée (see page 16)
1 tablespoon	Ground Roasted Coriander (see page 22)
½ teaspoon	chili powder
8 oz.	Boiled Onion Purée (see page 18)
1 teaspoon	salt or to taste

→ Bring half the milk to a boil, remove from the heat, and add the cashews and sunflower seeds. Leave to soak for 15–20 minutes, then purée until smooth in a blender.

→ Put the carrots and corn in a saucepan and add 15 fl. oz. water. Bring to a boil, then reduce the heat to medium and cook, uncovered, for 5 minutes.

→ Add the lemon juice and beans, then pile the cauliflower on top. Cover the pan and cook for an additional 5 minutes. Stir to reposition the vegetables halfway through.

→ Spread out the vegetables, along with their cooking liquid, in a large dish or roasting pan. This will prevent the vegetables from overcooking.

→ Heat the oil over low heat in a nonstick saucepan, about 12 inches in diameter, and add the caraway seeds, cinnamon stick, and cardamom pods. Allow the spices to sizzle gently for 20–25 seconds, then add the onion, and ginger and garlic purées. Increase the heat slightly and fry the ingredients for 5–6 minutes or until the onions are soft.

→ Add the ground coriander and chili powder, cook for 30 seconds, then stir in the onion purée and cook for 3–4 minutes.

→ Stir in the salt, the vegetables with all their cooking liquid, the blended cashew mixture, and the remaining milk. Bring to simmering point, then cook for 5 minutes, stirring once or twice. Serve with Saffron Rice (see page 176) and Beet Raita (see page 224).

Mung Bean and Watermelon Curry

Sabut Moong aur Tarbooz ki Kari

SERVINGS: 4
PREPARATION TIME: 15 minutes, plus soaking
COOKING TIME: 20 minutes
PER SERVING: Calories: 242; Fat: 6.4 g.; Saturated fat: 0.9 g.

Although mung beans need soaking for a few hours, they cook very quickly. Teamed with watermelon, they look striking and taste splendid. The watermelon releases its sweet juices into the beans, which are tossed in ginger, chilies, and cumin; a squeeze of lemon enhances the flavors.

8 oz.	mung beans, washed and soaked for 6–8 hours or overnight
¼	large watermelon, peeled and seeded
2 tablespoons	sunflower or canola oil
½ teaspoon	black mustard seeds
1 teaspoon	grated fresh ginger
1–2	green chilies, seeded and finely chopped
½–1 teaspoon	chili powder
½ teaspoon	ground turmeric
1 teaspoon	Ground Roasted Cumin (see page 21)
1¼ teaspoons	salt or to taste
1 teaspoon	sugar
5 fl. oz.	warm water
2 tablespoons	lemon juice

→ Drain the beans and put into a saucepan with 15 fl. oz. water. Bring to a boil and skim off the froth from the surface. Reduce the heat to medium and cook for 12–15 minutes or until the beans are tender. Stir to ensure that the beans cook evenly. Reduce the heat to low for the last 5 minutes. The beans should remain whole and the water should be reduced to about 2–3 tablespoons. Remove from the heat and set aside.

→ Cut the melon into 1-inch cubes, making sure you collect all the juices in a bowl as you do so.

→ Heat the oil over low heat in a saucepan. Add the mustard seeds and when they crackle, add the ginger and green chilies. Cook for 1 minute. Add the chili powder, turmeric, and half the cumin. Cook for 30 seconds.

→ Add the beans, watermelon, salt, and sugar. Increase the heat slightly and pour in the warm water. Cover and simmer for 4–5 minutes. Stir in the lemon juice and reserved cumin and remove from the heat.

→ Serve with boiled basmati rice and Dry-Spiced Okra (see page 202).

Spiced Lentils
Masala Dhal

SERVINGS: 4
PREPARATION TIME: 15 minutes
COOKING TIME: 40–45 minutes
PER SERVING: Calories: 240; Fat: 6.5 g.; Saturated fat: 0.8 g.

Red and green lentils are readily available and used in combination they look quite stunning. For a vegetarian menu, serve either Chapatis (see page 188) or rice and a vegetable dish as accompaniments. These lentils are also delicious with grilled fish, poultry, or meat.

4 oz.	red lentils
4 oz.	green lentils
2 tablespoons	sunflower or canola oil
1-inch piece	cinnamon stick, halved
1	small onion, finely chopped
2 teaspoons	Ginger Purée (see page 17)
2 teaspoons	Garlic Purée (see page 16)
1/2–1 teaspoon	chili powder
1/2 teaspoon	ground turmeric
1 teaspoon	salt or to taste
4 oz.	fresh tomatoes, skinned and chopped, or canned chopped tomatoes, drained
1 1/2 pints	warm water
2 tablespoons	chopped fresh cilantro leaves

Garnish

1	red chili, seeded and cut into julienne strips
1	green chili, seeded and cut into julienne strips

- ✦ Thoroughly wash both types of lentils together, then leave to drain in a colander.
- ✦ Heat the oil over medium heat in a nonstick saucepan. Add the cinnamon stick, onion, and ginger and garlic purées. Fry for 4–5 minutes, stirring frequently, until the onion begins to brown.
- ✦ Stir in the lentils, chili powder, turmeric, and salt. Fry for 3–4 minutes, stirring frequently, then add the tomatoes. Cook for an additional 2–3 minutes, stirring frequently.
- ✦ Pour in the water and bring to a boil. Reduce the heat to low, cover the pan, and cook for 25–30 minutes.
- ✦ Stir in the cilantro and cook, uncovered, for 1–2 minutes. Serve garnished with the red and green chilies.

Spiced Omelette Curry
Masala Umlet ki Kari

Servings: 4
Preparation time: 20 minutes
Cooking time: 15–20 minutes
Per serving: Calories: 135; Fat: 10.3 g.; Saturated fat: 2.3 g.

This is a low-fat version of a specialty among the Muslim community in the southern coastal region of India. The omelettes are cut into strips, then tossed in a lightly spiced tomato sauce. This dish is delicious with Puffed Grilled Bread (see page 194) or Chapatis (see page 188). A salad or a dry-spiced vegetable dish will complete the meal.

Omelettes

4	large eggs
2 tablespoons	finely chopped red onion
1	green chili, seeded and finely chopped
½ teaspoon	Ginger Purée (see page 17)
1 tablespoon	finely chopped fresh cilantro leaves
¼ teaspoon	ground turmeric
½ teaspoon	salt
a little	sunflower or canola oil for brushing pan

Sauce

1 tablespoon	sunflower or canola oil
½ teaspoon	ground turmeric
½ teaspoon	chili powder
½ teaspoon	salt or to taste
½ teaspoon	sugar
8 oz.	tomatoes, skinned and finely chopped
5 fl. oz.	warm water
1 teaspoon	Ground Roasted Cumin (see page 21)
1 tablespoon	finely chopped fresh cilantro leaves

→ Make two omelettes. Whisk the eggs with 2 tablespoons water until frothy (the water makes the omelettes light and fluffy). Add the remaining ingredients and mix thoroughly.

→ Brush a nonstick omelette pan, 5–6 inches in diameter, with sunflower or canola oil and place over medium heat. Pour half the egg mixture into the hot pan and stir the middle of the mixture gently, rotating it for even cooking.

→ Stop stirring and allow the egg to set, then turn the omelette over with a wide spatula. Cook the second side for 1–2 minutes. The omelette should resemble a thick pancake. Slide it out on to a board and cook the second omelette the same way.

→ Cut the omelettes into strips, about 1-inch wide, and cut the strips into 2-inch lengths. Set aside.

→ For the sauce, heat the oil over medium heat in a nonstick sauté pan. Add the turmeric, chili powder, salt, and sugar. Stir once, then add the tomatoes and cook for 3–4 minutes. Pour in the water, reduce the heat slightly and cook for an additional 3–4 minutes, stirring frequently.

→ Mix in the cumin and fresh cilantro, then add the omelette strips. Reduce the heat to low and cook for 2–3 minutes. Stir gently once or twice, then serve immediately.

Lentils with Hot Oil Seasoning
Tadka Dhal

SERVINGS: 4
PREPARATION TIME: 10 minutes
COOKING TIME: 30 minutes
PER SERVING: Calories: 200; Fat: 3.5 g.; Saturated fat: 0.5 g.

Tadka (or *tarka*) is a very popular and quick cooking technique used to add instant flavor to dishes. A selection of dried whole spices are usually used, with one or more fresh flavoring ingredients added. The choice of spices is regional—the following is typical of east and northeast India.

8 oz.	red lentils
1 teaspoon	ground turmeric
1 teaspoon	salt or to taste
1 tablespoon	sunflower or canola oil
$\frac{1}{4}$ teaspoon	black mustard seeds
$\frac{1}{4}$ teaspoon	fennel seeds
$\frac{1}{4}$ teaspoon	cumin seeds
$\frac{1}{4}$ teaspoon	onion seeds
6–8	fenugreek seeds
1–4	dried red chilies
2	bay leaves, crumpled
2 tablespoons	finely chopped fresh cilantro leaves

➔ Wash and drain the lentils, then place in a saucepan. Pour in 1½ pints water and add the turmeric. Bring to a boil, then reduce the heat to medium and cook, uncovered, for 5–6 minutes or until the foam subsides.

➔ Cover the pan and reduce the heat to low. Simmer for 20–25 minutes, then stir in the salt.

✦ In a small saucepan or a ladle, carefully heat the oil over medium heat. When hot, add the remaining ingredients, except the cilantro, and switch off the heat. Allow the spices to sizzle in the hot oil for 20–25 seconds, then pour this mixture over the cooked lentils.

✦ Stir in the cilantro and keep the pan covered until you are ready to serve the meal.

Healthy Hint

Lentils are ideal for a low-fat diet:
They're high in fiber and protein.

Rice and Bread

I N INDIA, RICE is considered to be the most valuable gift of nature and nearly half the population eats rice every day. Long-grain rice is the perfect partner for Indian dishes and basmati is the universally popular choice. While boiled rice and curry is the daily diet, pilaus and biryanis are cooked on special occasions.

Millions of years ago, early types of rice grew wild in parts of what is now southeast Asia, especially in water-logged fields. It was a form of grass, with miniature ears of grain at the top. Decades of cultivation and the use of natural organic fertilizers transformed the wild grass into the modern-day grain. Rice was first grown in northern Thailand and northeast India. Today, it is grown all over India and, because of the country's diverse geographical and climatic conditions, each region grows its own variety. The pride and joy of northern India is the exquisite basmati rice, which is the finest in the world. Southern India has its own variety of rice, known as *ambey mohur*, which has a subtle hint of mango fragrance (*ambey* meaning mango and *mohur,* fragrance).

Bread is another important daily food. Wheat and barley have been the staple grains in northern India since ancient times. Like rice, through natural evolution grains of wild grasses have been transformed into what we know as wheat. Everyday breads, and most other types of flat breads, are unleavened and made from whole wheat flour. Leavened breads, such as the different types of naan, were introduced to India by Middle-Eastern invaders.

Most flat breads are cooked on a cast-iron griddle known as a *tava*; a standard griddle or a heavy frying pan can be used, but it is easier to handle the bread if you use a pan without raised sides. In an Indian home, bread is freshly made for each meal and that is the way to enjoy it at its best. The dough can be stored in a plastic bag in the refrigerator for 2–3 days, then brought to room temperature for 30 minutes before rolling and cooking.

When making dough, add the water gradually because it is difficult to be precise about the quantity required. Some flours are more absorbent than others, so you may have to adjust the quantity of water suggested in the recipe. Use a little dry flour to dust each piece of dough before rolling out.

Do not be tempted to reheat Indian bread in the microwave. This ancient food isn't at all compatible with our modern miracle worker! The best method is to wrap the bread in aluminum foil and place in a preheated oven at 325°F. for 6–8 minutes. Overheating makes the bread brittle. Cooked bread can be frozen; thaw and reheat as for cooled bread.

Perfect Cooked Rice

Generally, you can cook rice by two simple methods. One is to boil the rice in plenty of water with a pinch of salt until the grains are tender, then drain it. This is fine for most long-grain rice, but basmati deserves a little special care to preserve its unique aroma and flavor. I prefer to cook basmati rice using the absorption method. Use the following simple rules and you will never be disappointed—they have never let me down!

➢ Weigh the quantity required accurately and wash the rice in cold water several times. The water will be cloudy for the first 2–3 changes of water, because of the starch in the rice. Wash the rice until the water runs clear, gently lifting and turning the grains, but do not rub them too hard.

➢ When the water is clear, soak the rice for 30 minutes, then drain it thoroughly in a colander.

➢ Use a saucepan that has a heavy base and isn't too small (basmati rice expands considerably during cooking). As a guide, the saucepan should be about two-thirds full when the rice is cooked.

➢ Measure the water accurately. Once the lid goes on the saucepan, set the timer and do not worry about the rice until the time is up. Do not be tempted to lift the lid—it is important to keep the steam in the pan.

➢ The heat level is important for the final cooking time: turn it down to simmering point and use a heat diffuser, if necessary, for gentle cooking. I have never found it necessary to cook basmati rice for longer than 10 minutes, except when it is cooked with meat, seafood, vegetables, or other ingredients.

➢ When the rice is cooked, remove the pan from the heat and let it rest for 8–10 minutes. Again, do not be tempted to uncover the pan. This is important because freshly cooked basmati rice is very fragile. Once it has had time to absorb the starch back into the grains, simply fluff up the rice with a fork and use a metal spoon to serve it.

Healthy Hint

Rice is an excellent food for babies and convalescents
because it is nourishing and easily digested.
Rice is also believed to cool the body. This is probably
the reason why rice is the staple food in the sultry southern
Indian climate, whereas bread is more popular in the cooler
north. Rice is a good source of carbohydrate, which is
an essential part of a healthy diet.

Cumin-Coriander Rice

JEERA-DHANIA CHAWAL

SERVINGS: 4
PREPARATION TIME: 5 minutes, plus soaking
COOKING TIME: 12–13 minutes
PER SERVING: Calories: 277; Fat: 3.5 g.; Saturated fat: 0.3 g.

When you have company, you may feel like cooking something special rather than boiled rice (although, to me, nothing beats the aroma of freshly cooked plain basmati). This recipe is a simple one with a fairly neutral background and the ideal complement for any curry or spicy grilled meat or poultry.

8 oz.	basmati rice, washed and soaked in cold water for 30 minutes
1 tablespoon	sunflower or canola oil
1 teaspoon	cumin seeds
1 teaspoon	coriander seeds, crushed
¼ teaspoon	ground turmeric
1 teaspoon	salt or to taste
16 fl. oz.	warm water
	fresh cilantro sprigs, to garnish

➜ Drain the rice and leave it to drain in a colander.

➜ Heat the oil in a nonstick saucepan over medium heat. Add the cumin seeds and coriander seeds and let them sizzle for 10–15 seconds.

➜ Add the rice, turmeric, and salt. Fry the rice, stirring constantly, for 2 minutes, then pour in the warm water. Bring to a boil, reduce the heat to low and cover the pan tightly.

➜ Cook, undisturbed, for 10 minutes. Remove from the heat and allow to rest for 8–10 minutes, then fluff up the rice with a fork. Serve garnished with fresh cilantro.

Cinnamon Rice

DALCHINI CHAWAL

SERVINGS: 4
PREPARATION TIME: 2–3 minutes, plus soaking
COOKING TIME: 10–12 minutes
PER SERVING: Calories: 227; Fat: 3.5 g.; Saturated fat: 0.3 g.

This is a simple recipe for boiled rice flavored with cinnamon and bay leaf. The Indian bay leaf comes from the cinnamon tree and it has a similar flavor to cinnamon. I have fond memories of plucking fresh cinnamon leaves for my mother and removing pieces of the bark to eat as a breath freshener!

8 oz.	basmati rice, washed and soaked in cold water for 30 minutes
1 teaspoon	sunflower or canola oil
½ teaspoon	salt or to taste
2-inch	piece of cinnamon stick
2	bay leaves, halved

→ Drain the rice and leave it to drain in a colander.

→ In a heavy saucepan bring 16 fl. oz. water to a boil. Add the remaining ingredients.

→ Add the rice and bring back to a boil. Reduce the heat to medium and cook for 4–5 minutes or until the surface water has almost evaporated. Reduce the heat to very low (use a heat diffuser, if necessary, for gentle cooking) and cover the pan tightly. If you do not have a tight-fitting lid, cover with a piece of aluminum foil first, then put the lid on the pan. Cook for 5 minutes.

→ Remove from the heat and leave the pan undisturbed for 6–7 minutes. Remove the cinnamon and bay leaves, fluff up the rice with a fork, and serve.

Saffron Rice

KESARI CHAWAL

SERVINGS: 4
PREPARATION TIME: 5–10 minutes, plus soaking
COOKING TIME: 10–12 minutes
PER SERVING: Calories: 227; Fat: 3.5 g.; Saturated fat: 0.3 g.

Although there are many versions of saffron rice, this recipe is rather special. It derives from the Mogul era and, as well as saffron, it has the irresistible, heady aroma of rose essence. Floral essences were first introduced during the Mogul period and they have been used in Indian cuisine for thousands of years.

8 oz.	basmati rice, washed and soaked in cold water for 30 minutes
1 tablespoon	sunflower or canola oil
4	green cardamom pods, bruised
1 teaspoon	caraway seeds
½ teaspoon	salt
16 fl. oz.	warm water
pinch	saffron threads, pounded
4–5	drops of rose essence
a few	fresh rose petals, washed and dried, to garnish

→ Drain the rice and leave it to drain in a colander.

→ In a nonstick saucepan, heat the oil over medium heat. Add the cardamom and caraway seeds and let the spices sizzle for 20–25 seconds.

→ Add the rice and fry for 2–3 minutes, stirring.

→ Add the salt and pour in the warm water. Bring to a boil and stir in the saffron and rose essence. Reduce the heat to low, cover the pan and cook for 8–10 minutes without lifting the lid. Remove from the heat and leave to stand, undisturbed, for 6–8 minutes.

→ With a metal spoon, transfer the rice to a serving dish, surround with the rose petals and serve.

 COOK'S TIP: Concentrated pure rose essence is available in Indian stores, but you could use 1½ tablespoons rose water, which you can buy from large supermarkets.

Fried Brown Rice

BHUNA HUA CHAWAL

SERVINGS: 4
PREPARATION TIME: 5 minutes, plus soaking
COOKING TIME: 15 minutes
PER SERVING: Calories: 270; Fat: 6 g.; Saturated fat: 0.7 g.

This is the traditional accompaniment for dhansak. Sugar is caramelized in hot oil before the rice is added along with a few whole spices. I find that it tastes just as good with other dishes, such as Lentils with Kidney Beans (see page 153) or Spiced Mixed Lentils (see page 156).

8 oz.	basmati rice, washed and soaked for 30 minutes
2 tablespoons	sunflower oil
4 teaspoons	sugar
4	green cardamom pods, bruised
1-inch	piece of cinnamon stick
2	cloves
1	bay leaf, crumbled
½ teaspoon	salt or to taste
16 fl. oz.	hot water

✤ Drain the rice and leave it in a colander to drain.

✤ In a nonstick saucepan, about 10 inches in diameter, heat the oil over medium heat. When hot, add the sugar and wait until it has caramelized.

✤ Reduce the heat to low, then add the spices and bay leaf. Let them sizzle for 15–20 seconds, then add the rice and salt. Sauté for 2–3 minutes.

✤ Pour in the water and bring to a boil. Boil steadily for 2 minutes, then reduce the heat to very low. Cover the pan and cook for 8 minutes.

✤ Remove the pan from the heat and let it stand for 8–10 minutes undisturbed, without lifting the lid. Fluff up the rice with a fork and serve.

Chicken Pilau

MURGH PULAO

SERVINGS: 4
PREPARATION TIME: 20–25 minutes, plus soaking
COOKING TIME: 25 minutes
PER SERVING: Calories: 445; Fat: 9 g.; Saturated fat: 2 g.

The delicate scent and flavor of basmati rice is characteristic of all pilaus. Basmati means fragrant, and this exquisite rice is grown extensively in the foothills of the Himalayas. Northern chefs have stretched their imagination to superlative heights and created an amazing range of recipes for pilau rice. This adaptation of one of these fine recipes, though cooked without using ghee, captures the traditional flavors. It is a real delight to the palate.

10 oz.	basmati rice
pinch	saffron threads, pounded
2 tablespoons	rose water
2 teaspoons	white poppy seeds
1 tablespoon	sunflower seeds
1–3	dried red chilies, chopped
15–20	black peppercorns
1 lb.	boneless chicken thighs, skinned and halved
2½ oz.	low-fat plain yogurt
2 teaspoons	Ginger Purée (see page 17)
2 teaspoons	Garlic Purée (see page 16)
1	onion, finely sliced
1 tablespoon	Ground Roasted Coriander (see page 22)
1 teaspoon	Ground Roasted Cumin (see page 21)
2-inch	piece of cinnamon stick, halved
6	green cardamom pods, bruised
6	cloves

1½ teaspoons	salt or to taste
18 fl. oz.	Aromatic Stock (see page 25) or hot water
1 tablespoon	flaked almonds, toasted

✦ Wash the rice in several changes of water and soak it for 30 minutes, then leave it in a colander to drain.

✦ Mix the pounded saffron with the rose water and set aside.

✦ Using a coffee or spice mill, finely grind the poppy seeds, sunflower seeds, chilies, and peppercorns. Set aside.

✦ In a nonstick saucepan, at least 12 inches in diameter, mix the chicken with the remaining ingredients except the salt, stock or water, and flaked almonds. Place the saucepan over high heat and stir until the chicken begins to sizzle. Cook for 6–7 minutes, stirring frequently.

✦ When the chicken begins to brown, add the ground ingredients, and the salt, then reduce the heat to medium. Continue to cook for an additional 2–3 minutes, then stir in the drained rice.

✦ Pour in the stock or water and bring to a boil, then cover the pan with a piece of aluminum foil and place the lid on top. Reduce the heat to low and cook, without lifting the lid, for 10 minutes.

✦ Remove the lid and foil, and sprinkle the saffron and rose water mixture randomly on the rice. Discard the foil and cover the pan with the lid, then leave it undisturbed for 8–10 minutes.

✦ Carefully transfer the pilau to a serving dish and garnish with the toasted almonds.

COOK'S TIP: To cook ahead, cook the pilau in advance to the end of step 5. Then complete the cooking just before you are ready to serve the meal.

Meatballs with Pilau Rice

KOFTA PULAO

SERVINGS: 4
PREPARATION TIME: 30 minutes, plus soaking
COOKING TIME: 30 minutes
PER SERVING: Calories: 415; Fat: 6 g.; Saturated fat: 1.5 g.

Traditionally, pulao is a rich dish with ghee, and nuts and raisins are often added. This version uses traditional spices, but it is cooked with yogurt rather than ghee.

1 lb.	ground chicken or turkey
2–3	garlic cloves, peeled and coarsely chopped
1-inch	cube of fresh ginger, peeled and coarsely chopped
1–2	green chilies, seeded and chopped
½ oz.	chopped cilantro, including the tender stalks
2 teaspoons	ground coriander
1½ teaspoons	Garam Masala (see page 23)
2 oz.	low-fat plain yogurt
1½ teaspoons	salt or to taste
1	small onion, coarsely chopped
1 pint	hot water
4	green cardamom pods
2 1-inch	pieces of cinnamon stick
4	whole cloves
10–12	black peppercorns
2	bay leaves, crumbled
½ teaspoon	ground turmeric
10 oz.	basmati rice, washed and soaked for 30 minutes
½ oz.	flaked almonds, toasted, to garnish

- Put the chicken in a food processor with the garlic, ginger, chilies, cilantro, ground coriander, garam masala, half the yogurt, and half the salt. Blend until smooth, then add the onion and process until the onion is fine, but not puréed. Shape the mixture into walnut-sized balls (koftas)—you should have about 28 meatballs.
- Pour the water into a heavy saucepan, place over high heat and add the remaining yogurt. Beat with a wire beater until blended, then add the cardamoms, cinnamon, cloves, peppercorns, bay leaves, and turmeric.
- Bring to a boil and add the meatballs a few at a time so that the water is kept at boiling point until they're all added. Cover the pan and reduce the heat to low. Simmer for 15 minutes. Stir once or twice after the first 7–8 minutes' cooking, by which time the meatballs will be firm and will not fall apart.
- Use a draining spoon to remove the meatballs; set aside and keep hot. Drain the rice and add it to the meat stock with the remaining salt. Increase the heat to high, bring to a boil and boil for 2–3 minutes, then reduce the heat to very low (use a heat diffuser, if necessary, for gentle cooking), cover tightly and cook for 8 minutes.
- Pile the koftas on top of the cooked rice and cover the pan. Cook for 2 minutes, then remove from the heat. Leave the pan undisturbed for 8–10 minutes.
- Using a flat metal or plastic spoon (a wooden spoon will squash the grains), gently stir the pilau to distribute the koftas. Turn out on to a serving dish and garnish with the toasted almonds. Serve with Spinach Raita (see page 222) and grilled pappadums.

Variation

Use lean ground pork or lamb instead of the chicken or turkey.

 COOK'S TIP: The meatballs can be made in advance and stored overnight in the refrigerator or frozen. The stock can also be prepared and chilled or frozen. Thaw both before using them in the pilau.

Rich Lamb Pilau

YAKHNI PULAO

SERVINGS: 6
PREPARATION TIME: 30 minutes, plus soaking
COOKING TIME: 1¼–1¾ hours
PER SERVING: Calories: 540; Fat: 15 g.; Saturated fat: 6.5 g.

*T*he Mogul Emperors were pampered by their ingenious chefs, who created exotic pilaus and biryanis. A product of the royal kitchens, the word *yakhni* means rich meat stock and, in the original version, a large amount of ghee was added when making the stock in which to cook the rice. Ghee isn't added to this version and the ingredients have been modified to reduce the fat content, but the result is still a wonderfully aromatic pilau with a lighter, fresher flavor. This pilau is a meal in itself—raita and grilled pappadums are all that is required by way of accompaniments.

1 lb.	basmati rice, washed and soaked for 30 minutes
pinch	saffron threads, pounded
2 tablespoons	rose water
2 2-inch	pieces of cinnamon stick, halved
6	green cardamom pods, bruised
6	cloves
1 teaspoon	salt or to taste
1 tablespoon	flaked almonds, toasted
1–2 tablespoon	Browned Sliced Onions (see page 19)

Stock

1 teaspoon	black peppercorns
2 tablespoons	coriander seeds
2 tablespoons	cumin seeds
1 lb.	lamb neck fillet, cut into 1-inch cubes
6	lamb chops or cutlets, trimmed of rind and excess fat

3 2-inch	pieces of cinnamon stick
8	green cardamom pods, bruised
2	brown cardamom pods, bruised
12	cloves
2	bay leaves
8	garlic cloves, lightly crushed
3-inch cube	fresh ginger, sliced
4 oz.	low fat plain yogurt
1 teaspoon	salt

➣ First make the stock. Using a coffee or spice mill, lightly crush the peppercorns, coriander seeds, and cumin seeds. You could also do this by putting the spices in a plastic bag and crushing them with a rolling pin. Tie the crushed spices in a piece of cheesecloth (similar to a bought bouquet garni).

➣ Put both cuts of meat and the spice bag in a large saucepan with all the remaining ingredients for the stock. Pour in 4 cups water and bring to a boil. Reduce the heat to low, cover the pan, and simmer for 1–1½ hours or until the meat is tender.

➣ Strain the stock through a sieve. Remove the spice bag, whole spices, bay leaves, ginger, and garlic. Hold the spice bag over the stock and squeeze it out to extract all the flavor. Press the garlic and ginger through a sieve into the stock. Mix well and set aside. You should have about 1¾ pints; if not, add water to make it up to that amount. Set the meat aside.

➣ Drain the rice in a colander. Mix the saffron with the rose water and set aside to soak.

➣ In a nonstick saucepan, about 12 inches in diameter, bring the stock to a boil. Add the cinnamon, cardamoms, cloves, rice, and all the reserved cooked meat. Stir in the salt and bring back to a boil.

➣ Allow to boil for 2 minutes, then reduce the heat to very low (use a heat diffuser, if necessary, for gentle cooking). Cover the pan with a piece of aluminum foil, then put the lid on. Cook for 8–10 minutes.

➣ Sprinkle the saffron and rose water randomly over the pilau. Re-cover and leave to stand for 8–10 minutes.

➣ To serve, turn out the pilau on to a serving dish and garnish with the toasted almonds and browned onions.

Eggplant Pilau
Brinjal Pulao

SERVINGS: 4
PREPARATION TIME: 15 minutes, plus soaking
COOKING TIME: 16–17 minutes
PER SERVING: Calories: 290; Fat: 11 g.; Saturated fat: 1 g.

Eggplant is one of my favorite vegetables. I am always fascinated by the fact that, when cooked, the flesh is transformed into a smooth, velvety texture, absorbing whatever flavor you add to it. This recipe is from the southern coastal area of India where coconut is often used to add a creamy richness. I have used white poppy seeds and sunflower seeds instead, to achieve a similar richness.

8 oz.	basmati rice, washed and soaked in cold water for 30 minutes
1	medium eggplant, about 10 oz.
2 tablespoons	sunflower or canola oil
2 2-inch	pieces of cinnamon stick, halved
4	green cardamom pods, bruised
4	cloves
1	medium onion, finely sliced
½ teaspoon	ground turmeric
1 teaspoon	salt or to taste
16 fl. oz.	hot water

Spice mix

2 teaspoons	white poppy seeds
2 teaspoons	sunflower seeds
2 teaspoons	coriander seeds
1–3	dried red chilies, coarsely chopped
½ teaspoon	black peppercorns

→ First grind the ingredients for the spice mix in a coffee or spice mill.

→ Drain the rice and leave it to drain in a colander.

→ Quarter the eggplant lengthwise. Cut each quarter in half, then into 1-inch cubes. Soak the cubes in cold water to prevent them from discoloring, adding salt if you wish, but don't forget to rinse them before cooking.

→ In a nonstick saucepan, at least 10 inches in diameter, heat the oil over low heat. Add the cinnamon, cardamoms, and cloves and cook gently for 15–20 seconds. Add the onion and increase the heat to medium. Fry for 6–7 minutes, stirring frequently, until the onion is lightly browned.

→ Add the ground spice mix and cook, stirring, for 1 minute.

→ Drain the eggplant cubes and add them to the pan along with the rice, turmeric, and salt. Mix thoroughly and pour in the hot water. Bring to a boil, then reduce the heat and cover the pan tightly. If you don't have a tight-fitting lid, put a sheet of aluminum foil over the pan before putting on the lid. Cook for 10 minutes, then remove from the heat and leave the pilau undisturbed for 10 minutes. Fork through and serve.

COOK'S TIP: The age-old practice of soaking eggplant in salt or salted water to remove bitterness doesn't strictly apply to modern eggplant. I rarely follow this method and find no trace of bitterness.

Vegetable Pilau
SUBZI PULAO

SERVINGS: 4
PREPARATION TIME: 15–20 minutes, plus soaking
COOKING TIME: 20 minutes, plus standing time
PER SERVING: Calories: 290; Fat: 6 g.; Saturated fat: 0.75 g.

This is a simple dish with a colorful appearance and fabulous flavors. For a wholesome and tasty vegetarian meal, serve it with a lentil dish; it is equally enjoyable with kebabs and a raita.

8 oz.	basmati rice, washed and soaked in cold water for 30 minutes
2 tablespoons	sunflower or canola oil
½ teaspoon	cumin seeds
1-inch	piece of cinnamon stick
4	green cardamom pods, bruised
2	cloves
1	red onion, halved and finely sliced
6 oz.	carrots, coarsely grated
4 oz.	fresh spinach, finely shredded or frozen leaf spinach, thawed and drained
1 teaspoon	salt or to taste
½ teaspoon	ground turmeric
6 fl. oz.	warm water

➤ Drain the rice and leave it to drain in a colander.

➤ Heat the oil in a nonstick saucepan over medium heat. Add the cumin seeds followed by the cinnamon, cardamoms, and cloves. Let the spices sizzle for 15–20 seconds, then add the onion and fry for 4–5 minutes or until the onion has softened.

➤ Add the carrots and spinach and increase the heat to high. Stir-fry for 2–3 minutes, then reduce the heat to medium and add the rice, salt, and turmeric. Fry for 2–3 minutes, stirring constantly, then pour in the warm water.

✦ Bring to a boil and allow to boil vigorously for 1 minute, then reduce the heat to low. Cover the pan and cook for 10 minutes. Do not lift the lid during this cooking. Remove the pan from the heat without lifting the lid and set it aside to stand, undisturbed, for 5–6 minutes before serving.

Chapatis
CHAPATIS

SERVINGS: Makes 16
PREPARATION TIME: 10–15 minutes, plus resting
COOKING TIME: 30 minutes
PER SERVING: Calories: 95; Fat: 1.5 g.; Saturated fat: 0.2 g.

In an Indian home, chapatis are the equivalent of a loaf of bread in the American household. These everyday breads, made with whole wheat flour, are nutritious and they're a good source of fiber. This is because the entire wheat kernel is ground into the flour. Oil isn't used in traditional recipes, but I find a little oil makes softer chapatis. Warm water, rather than cold water, also helps to give a softer texture.

14 oz.	chapati flour
1 teaspoon	salt
2 tablespoons	sunflower or canola oil
8½ fl. oz.	lukewarm water

Serve with . . .
   any curry dish.

+ In a large mixing bowl, mix the flour and salt. Add the oil and work it into the flour well, then gradually add the water and mix until a dough is formed. Do not worry if the dough seems a little sticky at first—the excess moisture is absorbed by the flour by the time the dough is ready.
+ Transfer the dough to a clean surface and knead it for 4–5 minutes. Alternatively, make the dough in a food processor. Cover the dough with a damp cloth and leave to rest for 30 minutes.
+ Divide the dough in half and cut each portion into 8 equal-sized balls. Flatten the balls into round cakes by rotating them between your palms and then pressing them down gently.
+ Dust a cake of dough lightly with chapati flour and roll out into a 6-inch disk. Keep the remaining cakes covered with a damp cloth.

→ Preheat a heavy cast-iron griddle or other suitable shallow pan over medium-high heat. Place a chapati on it and cook until bubbles begin to appear on the surface. Using a fish slice, turn it over and cook until the underside has brown patches. You can check this by gently lifting the chapati. Turn it over again and press the edges down. The chapati will puff up now. Cook until brown patches appear on the other side. Once the pan is well heated, you may need to turn the heat down slightly.

→ Wrap the chapatis in a sheet of aluminum foil lined with paper towels to keep hot until you finish cooking all of the dough.

COOK'S TIP: You can buy whole wheat chapati flour from Indian stores and store it in the same way as ordinary flour. Whole wheat bread flour can be used but it is coarser than atta and I find the chapatis turn out rather dry. A good compromise is to mix whole wheat flour and plain flour in equal quantities.

Spiced Chapatis
MASALA CHAPATIS

SERVINGS: Makes 16
PREPARATION TIME: 15–20 minutes, plus resting
COOKING TIME: 30 minutes
PER SERVING: Calories: 95; Fat: 1.5 g.; Saturated fat: 0.2 g.

These chapatis are seasoned with ground cumin and coriander, and chili powder to pep up their flavor. Chopped cilantro adds a fresh, zesty flavor to the spiced dough.

14 oz.	whole wheat chapati flour, plus a little extra for dusting
1 teaspoon	salt
1½ teaspoons	ground cumin
1½ teaspoons	ground coriander
½–1 teaspoon	chili powder
2 tablespoons	finely chopped cilantro
2 tablespoons	sunflower or canola oil
Approx. 8½ fl. oz.	lukewarm water

Serve with . . .
any curry dish.

→ Put the flour in a large bowl and add the remaining ingredients, except the oil and water. Mix well.

→ Add the oil and work it well into the flour. Gradually add the lukewarm water—the exact quantity will vary, depending on the absorbency level of the flour you are using. Do not worry if the dough appears a little sticky at first; the flour will absorb all the moisture when you knead it. Transfer the dough to a board and knead it for 4–5 minutes until it is soft and pliable. You can also make the dough in a food processor if you wish. Cover it with a damp cloth and leave to rest for 30 minutes.

→ Divide the dough in half and make 8 equal balls out of each piece. Flatten each ball to a smooth round cake by rotating it between your palms. Dust each cake lightly in flour and roll out to a 6-inch disk. While you are working on one, keep the remaining cakes covered with a damp cloth.

→ Preheat a heavy cast-iron griddle or other suitable shallow pan over medium-high heat. Place a chapati on it and cook until bubbles begin to appear on the surface. Using a thin spatula, turn it over and cook until the underside has brown patches. You can check this by gently lifting the chapati. Turn it over again and press the edges down. The chapati will puff up now. Cook until brown patches appear on the other side. Once the pan is well-heated, you may need to turn the heat down slightly.

→ Wrap the cooked chapatis in a sheet of aluminum foil lined with paper towels to keep hot until you finish cooking all of them.

Tandoori Bread

TANDOORI ROTI

SERVINGS: Makes 8
PREPARATION TIME: 10 minutes, plus proving
COOKING TIME: 15–20 minutes
PER SERVING: Calories: 200; Fat: 3 g.; Saturated fat: 0.4 g.

*R*oti is one of the basic breads baked in the tandoor. The original recipe is unleavened, and nothing other than plain water is used in the dough. It is delicious if you can eat it as it comes out of the oven, but the taste and texture are no longer exciting when the bread is cold, so for this reason I decided to change my recipe. Here is my version, which can be eaten hot or cold. It can also be frozen.

1 lb.	whole wheat self-raising flour, plus 1–2 tablespoons for dusting
½ teaspoon	salt
1 teaspoon	sugar
1 packet	easy-blend yeast
1 tablespoon	sunflower or canola oil
5 oz.	low-fat plain yogurt
8–10 fl. oz.	soda water

→ Put the flour, salt, sugar, and yeast in a large bowl and mix well.

→ Beat the oil and yogurt together and rub into the flour.

→ Gradually add the soda water and mix until a dough is formed. Don't worry if the dough feels sticky at this stage; the flour will absorb all the excess moisture when you knead it.

→ Transfer the dough to a board and knead it until it is soft and springy and no longer sticks to the board. You can also make the dough in a food processor if you wish, in which case you should mix the dry ingredients first.

→ Put the dough in a large plastic bag and tie it at the top with a twist tie. Place the bag in a warmed bowl and leave the dough to rise in a warm place for 1–1½ hours.

→ Preheat the oven to 450°F. Line a baking sheet with baking parchment or greased greaseproof paper.

→ Divide the dough into 8 equal portions. Rotate each portion between your palms to make a smooth round ball, then flatten it to a round cake. Dust it in a little flour and roll it out to a 4-inch disk. Place on the prepared baking sheet and bake on the top shelf of the oven for 9–10 minutes or until puffed and browned in patches.

Puffed Grilled Bread

PHULKAS

SERVINGS: Makes 20
PREPARATION TIME: 10–15 minutes, plus resting
COOKING TIME: 15–20 minutes
PER SERVING: Calories: 75; Fat: 1.2 g.; Saturated fat: 0.2 g.

A phulka is quite similar to a chapati. The same dough is used but it is cooked over an open flame. Traditionally, one side of the phulka is cooked very briefly to leave it undercooked and the other side is cooked fully. Indian housewives have this knack of placing the uncooked side directly on the burning gas, using a pair of tongs. The bread then puffs up beautifully, with a thicker layer at the bottom, a thin layer at the top and a hollow between the two. They're absolutely divine and must be eaten hot. The process of using an open flame needs practice, but do not despair, they can be cooked very successfully under a hot grill. In fact, I find it easier and quicker to use the grill.

1   quantity Chapati Dough (see page 188).

➤ Divide the dough in half and make 10 equal balls out of each piece. Flatten each ball into a smooth round cake by rotating it between your palms, then pressing down gently. Cover the dough cakes with a damp cloth, then start rolling and cooking the breads one at a time.
➤ Preheat the grill to high and place a grill pan, without the grid, approximately 5 inches away from the heat source. It is important that the grill pan is also preheated.
➤ Dust a flattened cake lightly with flour and roll it out to a 5-inch disk. Make sure that the surface of the bread is smooth without any holes or tears, otherwise it will not puff up.
➤ Preheat a heavy cast-iron griddle or other suitable shallow pan over medium-high heat and place the bread on it. Flip it over after about 20 seconds and allow the other side to cook until brown spots and patches appear. Lift it off gently and place under the grill. The bread will puff up within a few seconds. Wait until light brown patches appear on the surface, then gently remove it from the grill on a spatula. Once the griddle is heated to the right temperature (usually after you have made 2–3 phulkas), you can turn the heat down slightly.
➤ Wrap the cooked phulkas in a piece of aluminum foil lined with paper towels to keep them hot until you have finished making all the breads.

Side Dishes, Salads, and Relishes

ONSIDERING THAT THE majority of the population is vegetarian, it isn't surprising that Indian cooks excel in the art of creating imaginative vegetable dishes. An Indian diet generally consists of vegetable dishes, small quantities of meat, and rice or bread made of whole wheat flour for completely balanced eating.

These days we are extremely lucky to have an endless supply of all kinds of fruits and vegetables from all over the world. I have tried to include a wide range of vegetable recipes that are all quick and easy, as they should be for side dishes. They're simply spiced to enhance, rather than mask, the natural flavors of the main ingredients.

The Indian method of cooking vegetables is very sensible because they're usually cooked slowly in their own juices or their cooking liquid is always used in the sauces. This helps to retain water-soluble vitamins that are otherwise lost in the cooking water when vegetables are boiled and drained. Frozen vegetables have as much nutritional value as fresh. For speed and convenience I have used frozen vegetables in a number of recipes.

When buying vegetables, always make sure that they're as fresh as possible. Avoid any produce that is bruised or beginning to rot in places. If possible, cook fresh vegetables on the day you buy them; if not, wrap them in plastic food bags and store them in the refrigerator.

Salads and relishes are an integral part of any Indian meal. They aren't only cooling and an essential balance to the meal, but for the vast majority of the population, who are vegetarians, they're also a great source of protein. Raitas are always yogurt-based and they're sometimes called salads. When making raitas you can use any vegetables or fruits as long as they're absolutely fresh. In most cases I have offered serving suggestions for the salads and raitas, but they can be served with virtually any dish. The chutneys are ideal with snacks and finger foods.

Throughout India, raitas are made in the same way. The regional difference lies only in the spicing and seasoning. For instance, whereas in northern India raitas are flavored with roasted and ground cumin seeds and chili powder, in the south they're flavored with a hot oil seasoning containing mustard seeds, dried chilies, and curry leaves.

Yogurt is an excellent source of protein, iron, calcium, and thiamine. It is known to assist with gastrointestinal problems. It is given to invalids and used in weaning babies because it is easily digestible, nutritious, and, most important, free from harmful organisms.

Indian housewives still make yogurt at home. The yogurt used in India is usually made from buffalo milk, which is creamier than cow's milk. The result is a mild yogurt. Commercial yogurt is set in unglazed earthenware pots, which improves its flavor and texture. Do try to use low-fat yogurt with active cultures for the recipes in this section— I find it matches Indian yogurt very closely.

Savory Potato Mash
ALOO BHARTA

SERVINGS: 4
PREPARATION TIME: 30–35 minutes
COOKING TIME: 6–8 minutes
PER SERVING: Calories: 175; Fat: 4.6 g.; Saturated fat: 0.5 g.

*L*ightly mashed potatoes, seasoned with a hint of spice, are an excellent substitute for traditional Indian staples, such as rice and bread. I have tried serving these with several of the grilled and roasted dishes in this book and, along with the friends who also tasted the dishes, found the combination most enjoyable. The potatoes are equally good with Chapatis (see page 188) and meat or poultry dishes.

1 lb.	potatoes, boiled in their skins
1½ tablespoons	sunflower or canola oil
½ teaspoon	black mustard seeds
½ teaspoon	cumin seeds
1–2	green chilies, seeded and finely chopped
1	small red onion, finely chopped, about 2–3 tablespoons
½ teaspoon	salt or to taste
¼ teaspoon	ground turmeric
2–3 tablespoons	finely chopped cilantro

→ Peel and lightly mash the potatoes to a coarse texture so that there are some whole but small pieces left.
→ Heat the oil in a nonstick saucepan over medium heat and add the mustard seeds. As soon as they pop, add the cumin seeds. Add the chilies and onion and fry for 3–4 minutes, stirring frequently. Stir in the salt, turmeric, and cilantro, then cook for 1 minute.
→ Add the potatoes to the pan and stir until the spices and the potatoes are thoroughly mixed and heated through. Serve immediately.

Karnataka Potato Curry
BATATA SUKKHE

SERVINGS: 4–6
PREPARATION TIME: 15–20 minutes
COOKING TIME: 10–12 minutes
PER SERVING: Calories: 200; Fat: 5.3 g.; Saturated fat: 4 g.

*P*otatoes are one of nature's most amazing gifts. Not only are they good for us, with their carbohydrate and fiber content, but they also have a quality of absorbing flavors easily. Here is a simple, but fabulous, recipe from the district of Karnataka in the southern coastal region of India. It is a dry spiced dish (the word *sukkhe* means dry).

1 lb.	potatoes, cut into 1-inch cubes
1 teaspoon	salt or to taste
½ teaspoon	ground turmeric
1 tablespoon	channa dhal or yellow split peas
1–3	dried red chilies, broken up
2 teaspoons	coriander seeds
¼ teaspoon	fenugreek seeds
5 fl. oz.	reduced-fat coconut milk, heated
1 tablespoon	lemon juice

Serve with . . .

any type of bread or as an accompaniment to grilled or baked fish, poultry, or meat dishes.

→ Put the potatoes in a large saucepan, about 12 inches in diameter, and add 15 fl. oz. water, the salt, and turmeric. Bring to a boil, reduce the heat to low, and cover the pan. Cook for 6–7 minutes.

→ Meanwhile, preheat a small pan over medium heat. Add the channa dhal, chilies, coriander seeds, and fenugreek seeds. Reduce the heat to low and stir the mixture for 30–60 seconds or until the spices begin to release their aroma. Transfer the mixture to a plate and allow to cool slightly, then grind to a fine powder in a coffee or spice mill.

✦ Add the ground ingredients to the heated coconut milk. Stir until well blended, then add to the potatoes. Simmer, uncovered, until the potatoes are tender and all the liquid has been absorbed.

✦ Add the lemon juice and stir gently to mix it into the potatoes without breaking them up.

Spiced Sweet Potatoes
MASALEDAR SHAKURKANDI

SERVINGS: 4
PREPARATION TIME: 10–15 minutes
COOKING TIME: 15–18 minutes
PER SERVING: Calories: 200; Fat: 6 g.; Saturated fat: 0.8 g.

Sweet potatoes grow in warm climates, including India. There are many varieties and the type most common is pink skinned with lovely, moist orange-colored flesh.

1 lb.	sweet potatoes
2 tablespoons	sunflower or canola oil
2 teaspoons	Garlic Purée (see page 16)
½–1 teaspoon	chili powder
1 teaspoon	salt or to taste
½ teaspoon	Ground Roasted Cumin (see page 21)
1 teaspoon	Ground Roasted Coriander (see page 22)
2 tablespoons	finely chopped cilantro

➤ Preheat the oven to 400°F.

➤ Peel the sweet potatoes in the same way as ordinary potatoes. Cut them into bite-sized pieces, about ½-inch chunks. Wash and drain the pieces, then dry them thoroughly with a cloth.

➤ Heat the oil in a roasting tin until it is almost smoking. Add the potatoes, garlic purée, chili powder, and salt. Stir to mix thoroughly, then cook in the oven for 12–15 minutes, stirring two or three times to ensure the potatoes cook evenly.

➤ Sprinkle the cumin and ground coriander evenly over the potatoes and stir once. Continue to cook for an additional 2–3 minutes.

➤ Stir in the cilantro and serve immediately. The sweet potatoes are good with dishes like Chicken in Apricot Juice (see page 84) or Turkey in Orange Juice (see page 112) or with dry dishes, such as Baked Kebabs (see page 122).

COOK'S TIP: When you buy sweet potatoes, look for the ones that feel firm and store them with ordinary potatoes, in a cool dry place, away from direct light. Sweet potatoes should not be stored for longer than 7 or 8 days.

Healthy Hint

Sweet potatoes contain fiber, potassium, and vitamin C, and they're a rich source of vitamin E. The orange-fleshed variety is a good source of beta carotene, an antioxidant believed to help prevent cancer.

Dry-Spiced Okra
BHINDI BHAJI

SERVINGS: 4
PREPARATION TIME: 15–20 minutes
COOKING TIME: 13–15 minutes
PER SERVING: Calories: 140; Fat: 10.5 g.; Saturated fat: 1.4 g.

Cultivated in Africa, Egypt, and India, okra have beautiful white seeds inside their angular pods. When the vegetables are cut, the sticky seeds tend to make the dish slightly gelatinous, so I prefer to cook okra whole, except when I deep-fry them. Choose small tender okra for this recipe.

9 oz.	okra
2	small ripe but firm tomatoes, halved and seeded
1 tablespoon	sesame seeds
2 tablespoons	sunflower seeds
1 tablespoon	channa dhal or yellow split peas
1–3	dried red chilies, broken up
1½ tablespoons	sunflower or canola oil
½ teaspoon	cumin seeds
4–5	fenugreek seeds
1 teaspoon	Garlic Purée (see page 16)
½ teaspoon	salt or to taste

→ Wash the okra thoroughly and slice off the hard stalk end. Cut the tomato halves lengthwise into 3–4 pieces.

→ Preheat a small pan over medium heat. Add the sesame and sunflower seeds, channa dhal, and chilies. Reduce the heat slightly and roast the ingredients, stirring constantly, until the seeds are lightly browned and the dhal or peas have brown spots. Do not allow the seeds to darken. Transfer to a plate and allow to cool slightly, then grind to a smooth powder in a coffee or spice mill.

+ Heat the oil in a nonstick pan over low heat. Add the cumin seeds and let them sizzle for 15–20 seconds. Add the fenugreek seeds and garlic purée, and cook for 1 minute, stirring.

+ Thoroughly mix in the okra and salt. Cover the pan and cook for 8–10 minutes, stirring occasionally, until the okra is tender, but firm.

+ Add the ground ingredients and increase the heat to medium. Stir and cook for 1 minute, then add the tomatoes. Mix well and remove from the heat. Serve with any bread and dishes such as Dry-Fried Lamb (see page 120), Chicken Do-Piaza (see page 92) or Dry-Spiced Chicken Drumsticks (see page 96). For a vegetarian meal, serve with bread or rice, and a lentil or bean dish.

Carrots and Green Beans with Poppy Seeds
Gajjar aur Same

SERVINGS: 4
PREPARATION TIME: 15 minutes
COOKING TIME: 20–25 minutes
PER SERVING: Calories: 92; Fat: 8.7 g.; Saturated fat: 1 g.

This is a quick, tasty, and attractive side dish, which can be served with just about any curry and rice or bread. Poppy seeds are generally used to add richness and a nutty flavor, and to thicken sauces. In this recipe, they simply coat the vegetables, making them look and taste delectable.

2 tablespoons	white poppy seeds
1 tablespoon	sunflower seeds
1 tablespoon	sunflower or canola oil
½ teaspoon	black mustard seeds
½ teaspoon	cumin seeds
1–2	dried red chilies, roughly chopped
2	large garlic cloves, crushed
½ teaspoon	ground turmeric
12 oz.	carrots, cut into 2-inch strips (like French fries)
12 oz.	whole green beans, fresh or frozen, cut into 2-inch pieces
½ teaspoon	salt or to taste
5 fl. oz.	warm water

→ Preheat a small pan over medium heat. When hot, reduce the heat to low and add the poppy seeds and sunflower seeds. Stir them constantly for 1 minute until they're lightly browned. Do not allow them to darken. Transfer the seeds to a plate to cool, then grind them in a coffee or spice mill and set aside.

→ Heat the oil in a nonstick saucepan over medium heat. When hot but not smoking, add the mustard seeds. As soon as they start popping, reduce the heat to low and add the cumin seeds, chilies, and garlic. Stir-fry for 1 minute.

→ Add the turmeric, followed by the vegetables and salt. Increase the heat to medium and cook for 2 minutes, stirring constantly. Pour in the warm water, cover the pan, and reduce the heat slightly. Cook for 15–20 minutes or until the vegetables are tender, stirring occasionally and adding a little more water if necessary. The vegetables should be tender but firm and no water should be left in the pan.

→ Add the ground seeds and stir over medium heat for 1 minute. Remove from the heat and serve.

Cabbage with Ginger
Adraki Bandh Gobi

SERVINGS: 4
PREPARATION TIME: 15 minutes
COOKING TIME: 20–25 minutes
PER SERVING: Calories: 88; Fat: 3.5 g.; Saturated fat: 0.5 g.

This side dish can be rustled up in a jiffy and it is good with almost any meal. Ginger is the predominant flavor here—prepare it just before cooking to enjoy its warm, woody aroma that complements the sweet taste of the juicy green cabbage.

1 tablespoon	sunflower or canola oil
½-inch cube	fresh ginger, finely chopped or grated
1	red chili, seeded and sliced
1	red onion, finely sliced
¼ teaspoon	ground turmeric
1	small green cabbage, about 1 lb., finely chopped
4½ oz.	cooked fresh or frozen peas
½–1 teaspoon	salt

→ Heat the oil in a nonstick saucepan or sauté pan over medium heat and fry the ginger, chili and onion for 5–6 minutes or until the onion is lightly browned. Reduce the heat slightly halfway through cooking.

→ Stir in the turmeric, followed by the cabbage, peas, and salt. Mix well, then sprinkle 2 tablespoons water over the vegetables. Reduce the heat to low, cover the pan and cook for 15 minutes, stirring occasionally.

→ Cook, uncovered, if necessary, until the vegetables absorb all the cooking juices. Serve immediately.

Dry-Spiced Carrots with Peas
Gajjar aur Matar ki Bhaji

SERVINGS: 4
PREPARATION TIME: 15 minutes
COOKING TIME: 15 minutes
PER SERVING: Calories: 95; Fat: 3.8 g.; Saturated fat: 0.5 g.

Tender and juicy pieces of carrot combine with garden peas to make a delicious side dish in a jiffy. Cut the carrots into small pieces, each no more than double the size of a pea.

9 oz.	carrots, finely diced
1 tablespoon	sunflower or canola oil
½ teaspoon	black mustard seeds
½ teaspoon	cumin seeds
½ teaspoon	black pepper, coarsely crushed
1–2	red chilies, seeded and chopped
9 oz.	frozen peas
¼ teaspoon	salt or to taste
1 tablespoon	chopped cilantro
1 tablespoon	lemon juice
1 tablespoon	besan (graham or chickpea flour)

→ Put the carrots in a saucepan and add 10 fl. oz. water. Bring to a boil, reduce the heat to medium and cook for 8–10 minutes or until the carrots are tender, but firm. Remove the carrots with a slotted spoon and reserve the cooking water—you should have about 5 fl. oz. liquid.

→ Heat the oil in a nonstick saucepan over low heat. Add the mustard seeds, then, as soon as they start crackling, add the cumin seeds followed by the pepper and chilies. Cook for 30 seconds.

→ Return the carrots to the pan with the peas, salt, and reserved cooking liquid. Increase the heat to medium and cook, uncovered, for 5–6 minutes.

→ Reduce the heat to low again, then stir in the cilantro leaves and lemon juice. Using a fine sieve, sift the besan evenly over the vegetables. Stir until well blended and the vegetables are coated with the besan. Remove from the heat and serve as an accompaniment for any meat or fish curry.

Cauliflower with Green Chutney

HARIYALI GOBI

SERVINGS: 4
PREPARATION TIME: 25 minutes
COOKING TIME: 15–20 minutes
PER SERVING: Calories: 180; Fat: 10 g.; Saturated fat: 3 g.

*S*oft green coriander chutney looks quite spectacular on snow-white cauliflower florets and the combination is seriously delicious! The preparation and cooking could not be simpler.

1	large cauliflower
½ oz.	desiccated coconut
1	small red onion, coarsely chopped
½-inch cube	fresh ginger, coarsely chopped
2	large garlic cloves, coarsely chopped
½ oz.	cilantro leaves and stalks, coarsely chopped
½ teaspoon	salt
1 tablespoon	besan (gram or chickpea flour)
2 tablespoons	sunflower or canola oil
2–3	firm but ripe tomatoes, sliced
1–2	red chilies, seeded and cut into julienne strips

→ Blanch the cauliflower in salted water for 5 minutes. Drain and refresh in cold water, then cut into 3-inch diameter florets. Leave to drain thoroughly in a colander.

→ Preheat the oven to 425°F. Grind the coconut in a coffee grinder or spice mill until fine.

→ Put the remaining ingredients, except the tomatoes and chilies, into a blender. Add the coconut and 4 fl. oz. water, then blend until smooth.

- Put the cauliflower into a roasting tin and pour over the blended ingredients. Mix thoroughly and cook for 15–20 minutes, or until brown patches appear on the surface of the florets.
- Garnish with the tomatoes and chilies, and serve immediately. The cauliflower complements almost any fish, poultry, or meat dish.

Healthy Hint

Cauliflower provides vitamins C, B6, and folate.
It is very low in calories, which also makes it ideal for
anyone with a weight problem.

Mixed Vegetable Curry
Sabzion ki Kari

Servings: 4
Preparation time: 25 minutes
Cooking time: 20 minutes
Per serving: Calories: 200; Fat: 8 g.; Saturated fat: 6 g.

From south India, the characteristic flavors in this simple vegetable curry come from curry leaves and fenugreek seeds. It is good with fish, poultry, or meat dishes and it also makes a wholesome vegetarian meal when served with a lentil dish and rice or bread.

2 teaspoons	coriander seeds
1/4 teaspoon	fenugreek seeds
1 tablespoon	channa dhal
1–3	dried red chilies, chopped
14 oz.	potatoes, cut into 1-inch cubes
8 oz.	carrots, cut into 1-inch thick slices
1/4 teaspoon	ground turmeric
1/4–1/2 teaspoon	chili powder
8 oz.	tomatoes, skinned and chopped or canned chopped tomatoes, drained
1 teaspoon	salt or to taste
4 1/2 oz.	frozen peas
10–12	fresh or dried curry leaves
2 fl. oz.	reduced-fat coconut milk
2 fl. oz.	water

→ Preheat a small frying pan over medium heat. When hot, reduce the heat to low and add the coriander seeds, fenugreek seeds, channa dhal, and chilies. Roast the spices gently for 30–60 seconds, stirring, until they release their aroma. Transfer the spices to a plate and allow to cool, then grind them to a fine powder in a coffee grinder or spice mill.

→ Put the potatoes and carrots in a saucepan and add 15 fl. oz. water. Bring to a boil and stir in the turmeric and chili powder. Reduce the heat to low, cover the pan, and cook for 5–6 minutes.

→ Add the tomatoes and salt, re-cover and cook for 2–3 minutes, then add the peas and curry leaves.

→ Stir the coconut milk and water together, then add the mixture to the vegetables with the ground roasted ingredients.

→ Bring to a gentle simmer and cook, uncovered, for 6–8 minutes or until the vegetables are tender but firm. Remove from the heat and serve.

Spiced Green Beans
Farash Bean Masala

SERVINGS: 4
PREPARATION TIME: 10–15 minutes
COOKING TIME: 12–15 minutes
PER SERVING: Calories: 60; Fat: 5 g.; Saturated fat: 2.4 g.

This recipe works very well with either green or runner beans. If you use frozen beans, thaw them first, but reserve and use the water released during thawing for maximum nutritional value. This is another versatile side dish with subtle flavors that go with almost any main dish.

9 oz.	runner beans or green beans
2 teaspoons	lemon juice
1 tablespoon	sunflower or canola oil
½ teaspoon	black mustard seeds
½ teaspoon	cumin seeds
¼–½ teaspoon	crushed dried red chilies
½ teaspoon	salt or to taste
1 tablespoon	desiccated coconut

→ Trim the runner beans and cut them at a slant into ¼-inch slices. Cut green beans into 1-inch pieces.

→ Put the beans in a saucepan. Add 10 fl. oz. water and the lemon juice (this helps to preserve the fresh color of the beans). Bring to a boil, then reduce the heat to medium. Cover the pan and cook for 8–10 minutes or until the beans are tender, but still firm.

→ Heat the oil in a nonstick saucepan or sauté pan over medium heat. Add the mustard seeds, then, as soon as they pop, add the cumin seeds and the chilies.

→ Add the beans to the spices along with the cooking liquid left in the pan. Stir in the salt and coconut, then cook, uncovered, for 3–4 minutes or until most of the liquid has evaporated. The beans should be quite moist and the stock reduced to about 1 tablespoon. Remove from the heat and serve.

COOK'S TIP: You can buy crushed dried chilies from supermarkets and Indian stores, but it is more economical to grind dried red chilies coarsely in a coffee grinder or spice mill.

Leeks with Coconut
ULLI THOREN

SERVINGS: 4
PREPARATION TIME: 15–20 minutes
COOKING TIME: 25 minutes
PER SERVING: Calories: 108; Fat: 8.6 g.; Saturated fat: 4 g.

This is a quick and easy recipe from Kerala, the exotic spice land in southern India. The traditional recipe uses onions (there is no Indian name for leek, so the Indian title indicates that onions are used), but I have used leeks (or you could use a mixture of red and white onions instead) and added a small quantity of carrots for color. Curry leaves give most south Indian dishes their distinctive taste. If you do not have fresh or dried curry leaves, add a handful of cilantro leaves for a different flavor.

1½ tablespoons	sunflower or canola oil
½ teaspoon	black mustard seeds
1-inch cube	fresh ginger, peeled and grated
1–2	green chilies, seeded and cut into julienne strips
6–8	curry leaves, fresh or dried
1 lb.	leeks, halved lengthwise and finely sliced
4½ oz.	carrots, coarsely grated
1 oz.	desiccated coconut
1 teaspoon	salt or to taste

→ Heat the oil in a nonstick saucepan over low heat. Add the mustard seeds, then, as soon as they pop, add the ginger, chilies, and curry leaves. Cook gently for 1 minute, stirring.

→ Add the leeks, carrots, coconut, and salt. Stir and sprinkle 3 tablespoons water over the vegetables. Cover the pan and cook for 10 minutes. Add an additional 3 tablespoons water, cover and cook for an additional 10–12 minutes or until the vegetables are tender. Remove from the heat and serve.

COOK'S TIP: Wash leeks thoroughly before cooking. Dirt is often trapped between the layers and the best way of removing it is to wash the leeks under running water when they have been slit lengthwise. This rinses out trapped grit.

Healthy Hint

Leeks contain potassium and folate. Traditional herbalists
believe that leeks can help as a remedy for sore throat
and kidney stones.

Fruit Curry
Phalon ki Kari

SERVINGS: 4
PREPARATION TIME: 15–20 minutes
COOKING TIME: 25–30 minutes
PER SERVING: Calories: 315; Fat: 13 g.; Saturated fat: 7 g.

I have adapted this recipe from a hugely popular south Indian dish in which a selection of fresh and dried fruits are cooked in rich coconut milk extracted from fresh coconut. In this version I have used light coconut milk, which results in a lighter, fresher flavor. To make an exotic meal, serve with Saffron Rice (see page 176).

1 tablespoon	sunflower or canola oil
½ teaspoon	black mustard seeds
1-inch piece	cinnamon stick, halved
1 teaspoon	Ginger Purée (see page 17)
½ teaspoon	ground cumin
4½ oz.	fresh pineapple, cut into 1-inch cubes
1 teaspoon	salt or to taste
3 oz.	sugar or to taste
½–1 teaspoon	chili powder
5 fl. oz.	warm water
1 oz.	unroasted cashew nuts
4½ oz.	ready-to-eat dried apricots
1	eating apple
1	small, very firm banana
1 oz.	raisins
2 fl. oz.	reduced-fat coconut milk, blended with 2 fl. oz. water
1–2	green chilies, seeded and finely chopped
12–15	dried or fresh curry leaves

Garnish

| 1–2 tablespoons | low-fat sour cream |
| about 3 | glacé cherries, cut into slivers, rinsed and dried |

→ Heat the oil in a medium nonstick saucepan over low heat. When the oil is hot but not smoking, add the mustard seeds. As soon as they start popping, add the cinnamon stick and ginger purée and fry for 1 minute, stirring.

→ Add the cumin and fry for 15–20 seconds, then add the pineapple, salt, sugar, and chili powder. Pour in the warm water, bring to a boil, and reduce the heat to medium. Cover and cook for 6–7 minutes.

→ Add the cashews and apricots, re-cover and cook for an additional 6–8 minutes.

→ Meanwhile, peel and core the apple and cut it into 1-inch cubes. Cut the banana into thick diagonal slices. Add the apple, banana, raisins, and coconut milk to the pan. Bring to a slow simmer and add the chilies and curry leaves. Cook, uncovered, for 8–10 minutes or until all the fruits are tender but still firm.

→ Transfer to a serving dish and swirl the sour cream over the top. Garnish with the cherries and serve.

Fruit Raita

PHALON KA RAITA

SERVINGS: 4
PREPARATION TIME: 15 minutes
PER SERVING: Calories: 80; Fat: 0.5 g.; Saturated fat: 0.3 g.

Raitas are served all over India as a cooling agent and an essential balance to a meal. The regional variation lies only in the flavoring used. In northern India, for example, the favorite way to add zest to a raita is by adding dry-roasted crushed cumin seeds and a little chili. In this recipe I have used seedless grapes and raisins, a popular combination of the Mogul era, but you can use any ripe fruit you like.

1 oz.	raisins
5 oz.	seedless green grapes
1	small ripe pomegranate
6 oz.	low-fat plain yogurt
½ teaspoon	sugar
½ teaspoon	salt
½ teaspoon	chili powder
½ teaspoon	Ground Roasted Cumin (see page 21)

Serve with . . .

any pilau, or with grilled meat, poultry or kebabs.

+ Soak the raisins in boiling water for 10 minutes, drain and cool.
+ Quarter or halve the grapes according to their size.
+ Cut the pomegranate in half. Place one half on a flat surface and hold it, seeds side down, with one hand. Tap all around the shell with the handle of a knife or other similar object (this loosens the seeds and makes it easier to remove them), then remove the seeds by pressing down the shell. Remove any white membrane that is still attached to the seeds. Repeat with the other half.
+ In a bowl, beat the yogurt until smooth. Add the sugar, salt, half the chili powder, and half the cumin, and mix well.

→ Add the raisins and grapes, and all but 1 tablespoon of the pomegranate seeds. Mix well and transfer the raita to a serving dish.
→ Sprinkle the remaining chili powder and cumin over the raita and garnish with the remaining pomegranate seeds.

Healthy Hint

Grapes and raisins are great energy boosters.
They're also rich in vitamins A, B, and C,
as well as potassium.

Pineapple Raita
Ananas ka Raita

SERVINGS: 4
PREPARATION TIME: 15 minutes
PER SERVING: Calories: 110; Fat: 6.5 g.; Saturated fat: 4 g.

*F*resh pineapple is ideal for this raita, but it can be quite sharp in taste unless you can find a fruit that is really ripe and sweet. It is difficult to be precise about the quantity of sugar needed for fresh pineapple. Drained canned pineapple is a good alternative and it doesn't need extra sugar when canned in syrup but if using fruit canned in natural juice add sugar to taste.

8 oz.	low-fat plain yogurt
1 oz.	desiccated coconut, ground to a fine powder in a coffee grinder
½–1 teaspoon	salt
	confectioner's sugar to taste
½ teaspoon	Ground Roasted Cumin (see page 21)
½ teaspoon	chili powder
8 oz.	pineapple, fresh or canned, peeled or drained, as necessary, and cubed
2 teaspoons	sunflower or canola oil
½ teaspoon	black mustard seeds

→ In a mixing bowl, beat the yogurt with a fork until smooth and stir in the coconut, salt, and sugar.
→ Reserve a little of the cumin and chili powder, then add the remainder to the yogurt with the pineapple. Mix well.
→ In a small saucepan, heat the oil over medium heat and add the mustard seeds. As soon as they pop, remove from the heat and pour over the raita. Mix well and serve sprinkled with the reserved cumin and chili powder.

Healthy Hint
Fresh pineapple is a good source of vitamin C.

Banana Raita
KELA KA RAITA

SERVINGS: 4
PREPARATION TIME: 10 minutes, plus chilling
PER SERVING: Calories: 95; Fat: 0.6 g.; Saturated fat: 0.4

This raita bursts with rich aroma and flavor. Tart lemon juice, sweet raisins and bananas, and the warm, assertive flavor of roasted cumin are perfectly balanced by a hot undertone of chili. This raita is divine with oily fish, such as mackerel, or rich meat, such as Goan Pork Curry (see page 134) or Baked Kebabs (see page 122). Select ripe bananas that are quite firm, with a hint of green on the skin.

8 oz.	low-fat plain yogurt
1/2 teaspoon	salt
1/2 teaspoon	Ground Roasted Cumin (see page 21)
1/2 teaspoon	chili powder
1 oz.	raisins
2	large ripe, firm bananas
1 tablespoon	lemon juice
pinch	coarsely ground black pepper
1/2 teaspoon	paprika

→ In a mixing bowl, beat the yogurt with a fork or wire whisk until smooth.
→ Add the salt, cumin, chili powder, and raisins. Mix well.
→ Peel the bananas and quarter them lengthwise. Chop into bite-sized pieces and sprinkle with lemon juice, then mix well. Gently fold the bananas into the yogurt mixture. Cover and chill for 1 hour.
→ Transfer to a serving dish, sprinkle with black pepper and paprika, and serve.

Healthy Hint
Bananas have plenty of potassium, which helps muscles and nerves to function efficiently. This mineral also regulates blood pressure. Their natural sugar content makes them a good source of energy and, in India, bananas are given to babies and adults as a cure for diarrhea because of their cellulose content.

Spinach Raita
Palak Raita

SERVINGS: 4
PREPARATION TIME: 10 minutes, plus cooling
COOKING TIME: 8–10 minutes
PER SERVING: Calories: 50; Fat: 1 g.; Saturated fat: 0.4 g.

*f*lavored with fresh ginger and roasted cumin seeds, this makes a delicious side dish. The vitamins and minerals present in spinach combined with the healthy properties attributed to yogurt make up a simple, healthy dish.

9 oz.	fresh spinach, chopped
2	round slices of fresh ginger
1 teaspoon	cumin seeds
10–12	black peppercorns
8 oz.	low-fat plain yogurt
½ teaspoon	salt
½ teaspoon	sugar

Serve with . . .

any curry and rice or bread. This raita is excellent with pilaus and biryanis.

- → Put the spinach, 4 fl. oz. water, and ginger in a saucepan and bring to a boil. Reduce the heat slightly and cook, uncovered, for 8–10 minutes or until the water evaporates. Remove from the heat and cool thoroughly.
- → Meanwhile, preheat a small heavy pan over medium heat and add the cumin seeds and peppercorns. Stir for about 30 seconds or until the spices release their aroma. Transfer to a plate to cool slightly, then crush the spices in a mortar with a pestle.
- → Beat the yogurt with a fork until smooth and stir in the salt and sugar. Discard the ginger and add the spinach to the yogurt along with the crushed spices.

Healthy Hint

Spinach provides vitamins A, B, and C, as well as potassium. Although spinach contains iron, because it also contains oxalic acid, much of the spinach is unavailable to the body, so it isn't a particularly good source of iron in the diet. Research suggests that spinach may be beneficial in preventing certain types of cancer and in treating high blood pressure.

Beet Raita

CHUKANDER KA RAITA

SERVINGS: 4
PREPARATION TIME: 10 minutes
PER SERVING: Calories: 60; Fat: 0.5 g.; Saturated fat: 0.3 g.

When mixed with cooked beets, plain yogurt goes through a magical transformation in flavor as well as color. The sweet, slightly earthy taste of beets is the perfect match for the slightly tangy yogurt.

8 oz.	low-fat plain yogurt
½ teaspoon	salt
½ teaspoon	sugar
1	green chili, seeded and finely chopped
1 tablespoon	cilantro, finely chopped
1 teaspoon	Ground Roasted Cumin (see page 21)
9 oz.	cooked beets, finely chopped
3–4	lettuce leaves, finely shredded

➔ In a mixing bowl, beat the yogurt until smooth and add the salt, sugar, chili, cilantro and half the cumin. Mix thoroughly.

➔ Stir in the beets until thoroughly combined.

➔ Line a serving dish with shredded lettuce and pile the beet raita on top. Sprinkle with the reserved cumin. Serve chilled or at room temperature.

Healthy Hint

Beets are rich in fiber and potassium. In India, beet leaves
are cooked as a vegetable as they contain essential vitamins
and minerals such as beta carotene, calcium, and iron.

Almond Chutney
BADAM KI CHUTNEY

SERVINGS: 4–6
PREPARATION TIME: 10 minutes, plus soaking and chilling
PER SERVING: Calories: 100; Fat: 7 g.; Saturated fat: 0.6 g.

Almonds are highly prized in Indian cooking, especially in the north. Beautiful almond blossoms herald the onset of spring in the northern state of Kashmir, where the nuts grow in abundance. This chutney has a rich, yet refreshing, flavor and can be made in a jiffy; it also keeps well for 5–6 days in an airtight container in the refrigerator.

2 oz.	blanched almonds
1	green eating apple, such as Granny Smith
1½ tablespoons	lemon juice
2 tablespoons	chopped cilantro and stalks
12–15	fresh mint leaves
1	green chili, seeded and chopped
½ teaspoon	salt
1 teaspoon	sugar
2 oz.	low-fat plain yogurt

➤ Put the almonds in a small bowl and add enough boiling water to cover them. Set aside for 15 minutes, then drain.
➤ Peel, core, and coarsely chop the apple. Mix with the lemon juice and put into a blender with the almonds and the remaining ingredients. Blend until smooth.
➤ Chill the raita for 1 hour before serving as a dip, with any finger food, or as a side dish.

Healthy Hint
Almonds provide protein, iron, and potassium. As they're high in calories, you should only eat them in small quantities. As well as being a tasty snack, apples are low in fat and calories, and a good source of vitamin C.

Date and Raisin Chutney

Khajur aur Kishmish ki Chutney

Servings: 4
Preparation time: 10 minutes, plus soaking
Per serving: Calories: 85; Fat: 0.11 g.; Saturated fat: 0.02 g.

Unlike its cooked Western counterpart, Indian chutney is made by grinding all the ingredients together to a smooth purée. This chutney is a real treat for its fabulous combination of sweet, savory, hot, and sour accents. It will keep for 2–3 weeks in an airtight jar in the refrigerator.

4 oz.	stoned dates, chopped
2 oz.	raisins
7½ fl. oz.	boiling water
1¾ teaspoons	chili powder
2¼ teaspoons	Ground Roasted Cumin (see page 21)
2 teaspoons	tamarind concentrate or 3 tablespoons tamarind juice
2 teaspoons	soft brown sugar
1½ teaspoons	salt
1 tablespoon	low-fat plain yogurt

→ Soak the dates and raisins in the boiling water for 30 minutes.
→ Reserve ½ teaspoon each of the chili powder and cumin and place the remainder in a blender. Add the remaining ingredients except the yogurt.
→ Add the dates and raisins to the blender with the water in which they were soaked. Blend until smooth.
→ Transfer the puréed mixture to a serving dish and swirl the yogurt on top. Sprinkle with the reserved chili powder and cumin, and serve.

Healthy Hint

Raisins are a concentrated source of energy and they also contain potassium and iron. Dried dates have a high concentration of potassium.

Fresh Tomato Chutney

TAMATAR KI CHUTNEY

SERVINGS: 4–8
PREPARATION TIME: 10 minutes, plus cooling
COOKING TIME: 5–6 minutes
PER SERVING: Calories: 45; Fat: 2 g.; Saturated fat: 0.25 g.

This tomato chutney is easy to make and it is delicious with all kinds of snacks. It will keep well in the refrigerator in an airtight container for up to 10 days.

12 oz.	tomatoes, chopped
1 tablespoon	sunflower or canola oil
1	onion, chopped
2	large garlic cloves, chopped
2	green chilies, seeded and chopped
2 teaspoons	ground cumin
1 teaspoon	salt
1 tablespoon	sugar or to taste
1 tablespoon	finely snipped fresh chives

✦ Put the tomatoes in a small saucepan. Cook, uncovered, over medium heat for 5–6 minutes or until the tomatoes are soft. Remove from the heat and leave to cool.

✦ Meanwhile, heat the oil over medium heat and fry the onion and garlic, stirring constantly, for 3–4 minutes.

✦ Add the chilies and cumin and cook for 30–40 seconds.

✦ Purée the tomatoes, onion mixture, salt, and sugar in a blender or food processor. Transfer to a serving dish, cool thoroughly and stir in the chives.

✦ Serve chilled.

Healthy Hint

Tomatoes are high in vitamins, particularly beta-carotene
from which vitamin A is generated, and potassium.
Research suggests that antioxidants present in tomatoes
help to reduce the risk of cancer and heart disease.

Fresh Vegetable Pickle
Achar Subz

SERVINGS: 6–8
PREPARATION TIME: 15–20 minutes
COOKING TIME: 10 minutes
PER SERVING: Calories: 8; Fat: 0.15 g.; Saturated fat: 0.02

This pickle is very similar to piccalilli, which originated in colonial India. This is a south Indian version, in which lemon or lime juice is used instead of vinegar.

2 teaspoons	salt
1 teaspoon	sugar
1/2-inch cube	fresh ginger, peeled and grated
1–2	green chilies, seeded and finely chopped
1/2 teaspoon	ground turmeric
1/2 teaspoon	asafetida (see "Healthy Hint" below)
1/4–1/2 teaspoon	chili powder
1 tablespoon	cornmeal
2 teaspoons	English mustard
2 tablespoons	lemon juice
6 oz.	cauliflower, cut into very small florets, about 1/8 inch
6 oz.	carrots, very finely chopped
4 1/2 oz.	French-cut green beans, finely chopped

Serve with . . .
any tandoori dish, grilled or baked meat, poultry, and fish.

➔ Put the salt and sugar in a medium saucepan and add 8 fl. oz. water. Bring to a boil, then boil for 5 minutes.

➔ Reduce the heat to low and stir in the ginger, green chilies, turmeric, asafetida, and chili powder.

→ Blend the cornmeal to a smooth paste with a little cold water and add to the pan with the mustard. Cook, stirring, until the sauce has thickened, then add the lemon juice, and remove from the heat.

→ Put the vegetables in a heatproof bowl and add the sauce. Mix and cool.

→ Leave the pickle at room temperature for 24 hours, then transfer to an airtight container and chill until required.

COOK'S TIP: My favorite meal combination is a bowl of freshly cooked basmati rice, cold tandoori chicken, and this pickle. The pickle can be served right away, but it tastes better if it is allowed to mature for at least 24 hours. You can store it in the refrigerator for up to 2 weeks.

Healthy Hint

Asafetida has digestive and disinfectant properties. In Indian cooking it is used in those difficult-to-digest dishes, such as deep-fried snacks, and dishes containing lentils or beans. You can find it in lumped or powdered form in Indian grocery stores.

Cabbage Salad
BANDHGOBI SALAT

SERVINGS: 4
PREPARATION TIME: 10–15 minutes, plus chilling
PER SERVING: Calories: 52; Fat: 2.7 g.; Saturated fat: 8 g.

White cabbage is best for this salad. You can also use the heart of a green cabbage, especially spring cabbage, but remove most of the outer leaves.

½ oz.	desiccated coconut
1 fl. oz.	hot water
10 oz.	white cabbage, finely shredded
1	green chili, seeded and finely chopped
1	small red onion, finely chopped
1 tablespoon	finely chopped cilantro
1 tablespoon	lemon juice
½ teaspoon	salt or to taste
4–6	cherry tomatoes, halved

❖ In a small bowl, mix the coconut with the hot water and set aside for 10 minutes.
❖ In a large mixing bowl, mix the remaining ingredients, except the salt and cherry tomatoes. Add the coconut (with any liquid) and mix well. Cover the bowl and chill for 1 hour.
❖ Stir in the salt and transfer the salad to a serving dish. Garnish with the cherry tomatoes and serve.

Healthy Hint
Cabbage is high in vitamins and low in calories. Raw cabbage is an excellent source of vitamin C and also contains beta-carotene, fiber, calcium, and potassium.

Cucumber and Peanut Salad

KAMANG KAKDI

SERVINGS: 4
PREPARATION TIME: 10–15 minutes
COOKING TIME: none
PER SERVING: Calories: 130; Fat: 11 g.; Saturated fat: 5 g.

This is a recipe from the simple, but exciting and extensive, repertoire of the Saraswat community in the Karnataka district of southern India. The cool, crisp cucumber, hot undertone of the green chili, sweetness of coconut, and tartness of lime juice is superlative, and roasted peanuts add crunchiness.

2	tablespoons desiccated coconut
2 oz.	roasted peanuts
12 oz.	cucumber, finely chopped
1½ tablespoons	lime juice
1 tablespoon	very finely chopped cilantro
1	green chili, seeded and finely chopped
½ teaspoon	salt or to taste
½ teaspoon	sugar

➤ Grind the coconut in a spice or coffee mill to a smooth powder. Coarsely crush the peanuts.
➤ Mix all the ingredients together and serve.

 COOK'S TIP: You can prepare this salad in advance, but do not add the peanuts, salt, and sugar until just before serving.

Kohlrabi Salad
KOHLRABI SALAT

SERVINGS: 4
PREPARATION TIME: 10–15 minutes, plus cooling
COOKING TIME: 7–8 minutes
PER SERVING: Calories: 99; Fat: 4.6 g.; Saturated fat: 3.5 g.

*I*f you have never cooked or eaten kohlrabi before, this is the recipe to try. It is easy to cook, delicious and healthy. You can buy kohlrabi from all good supermarkets. Peel and cut it just like a turnip.

1	kohlrabi, about 9 oz.
2	carrots, about 6 oz., diced into ¼-inch pieces
½-inch cube	fresh ginger, peeled and grated
1	green chili, seeded and finely chopped
½	teaspoon salt
½	teaspoon sugar
1 oz.	desiccated coconut
8 oz.	low-fat plain yogurt
½ teaspoon	Ground Roasted Cumin (see page 21)
½ teaspoon	chili powder or paprika

Serve with . . .
shredded lettuce leaves.

➜ Slice off both ends of the kohlrabi, peel and cut into ¼-inch cubes. Place in a saucepan.
➜ Add the carrots, ginger, and 5 fl. oz. water. Bring to a boil, reduce the heat to medium, cover the pan and cook for 3–4 minutes. Remove the lid and continue to cook for 4–5 minutes. The vegetables should be *al dente,* tender but with bite.

→ Remove the vegetables with a slotted spoon and set aside. Boil the cooking water until it is reduced to half its original volume. Stir in the chopped green chili, salt, and sugar and remove from the heat. Leave to cool.

→ Meanwhile, grind the coconut in a coffee grinder or spice mill to a smooth powder. Stir the coconut into the cooled liquid and transfer to a mixing bowl. Add the yogurt and whisk until smooth.

→ Add half the cumin and the cooked vegetables. Mix well and transfer to a serving dish. Serve chilled or at room temperature, sprinkled with the remaining cumin and chili powder or paprika, and surrounded by shredded lettuce.

Healthy Hint

Kohlrabi is rich in potassium and vitamin C.
It is also a source of both soluble and insoluble fiber
(the former is believed to be helpful in
lowering blood cholesterol).

Desserts

THE CUSTOM OF serving dessert isn't common in India, where sweet specialties are served only on festive occasions, such as at weddings. Dairy products are the main ingredients for traditional Indian desserts, which combine alluring colors, flavors, and textures, and most are delicately scented with rose or Kewra (screwpine) essences. On a daily basis, fruit is usually eaten after a meal, which isn't just healthier, but also refreshing after spicy food.

I have developed a few dessert recipes based on fruit, one of nature's greatest gifts. Low-calorie fruit is vital in a healthy diet, providing vitamin C and other valuable antioxidants. Many types also provide plenty of fiber. The recipes that follow suit the principles of healthy eating and are quick and easy to make—in fact, they're perfect to round off a spicy meal.

Mango Dessert
Aam ka Mitha

SERVINGS: 4–5
PREPARATION TIME: 10–15 minutes, plus soaking and chilling
PER SERVING: Calories: 300; Fat: 19 g.; Saturated fat: 11 g.

This delectable dessert is deceptively easy to prepare. Buy ready-to-use mango purée from Indian stores or purée drained canned mango and sweeten it to taste.

1½ oz.	unroasted cashew nut pieces
1 oz.	raisins
½ teaspoon	saffron threads, pounded
2½ fl. oz.	reduced-fat milk
1	ripe fresh mango
1 lb.	sweetened mango purée
5 fl. oz.	fat-free half-and-half
1 tablespoon	cornmeal
5 fl. oz.	low-fat sour cream
¼ teaspoon	nutmeg

→ Put the cashews and raisins in a bowl. Place the saffron in a small saucepan and add the milk. Bring to a boil, then pour the saffron-infused milk over the cashews and raisins. Cover and set aside for 15–20 minutes.

→ Carefully peel the mango with a sharp knife and slice off the flesh from either side of the central, large, flat stone, then remove the two thinner slices on the ends. Use a sawing action when cutting to avoid squashing the flesh, which is smooth, silky and quite delicate. Cut the slices lengthwise into thin slithers and set aside.

→ Mix the mango purée with the half-and-half in a saucepan. Blend the cornmeal to a smooth paste with a little water, then stir it into the mango mixture. Stir over low heat until thickened, but do not allow the mixture to boil. Remove from the heat and stir in the low-fat sour cream, saffron-flavored milk, along with the cashews and raisins and most of the fresh fruit, reserving some for decorating the dessert. Allow to cool completely.

→ Transfer the cooled mango mixture to a serving dish or individual stemmed glasses. Decorate with the reserved mango and chill for several hours. Sprinkle with nutmeg and serve.

Healthy Hint

Mango is easy to digest and is rich in beta-carotene
and vitamin C—two antioxidants that boost
the body's immune system.

Melon and Mango Dessert

Tarbooz aur Aam ka Mitha

SERVINGS: 4–5
PREPARATION TIME: 15–20 minutes
PER SERVING: Calories: 140; Fat: 0.88 g.; Saturated fat: 0.33 g.

Mango is India's most cherished fruit. The season is short and when it starts there is a certain euphoria among traders and consumers alike. Indian mangoes aren't sold in most supermarkets, but there is a regular stock of other varieties. Indian markets sell mangoes imported from India from May to July. Mango and watermelon is a stunning combination in this simple dessert, which is cooling and delicious, and looks rather spectacular.

1	watermelon
14 oz.	sweetened mango purée
¼ teaspoon	grated nutmeg
½ teaspoon	ground cinnamon
½ teaspoon	ground ginger
1–2 tablespoons	confectioner's sugar
a few	fresh mint leaves to decorate

→ Cut the melon in half, remove the seeds and scoop out the flesh with a melon baller, discarding the seeds in the flesh as you work.

→ Mix the mango purée with the nutmeg, cinnamon, and ginger. Taste, then add the sugar if necessary. Pour it into a shallow serving dish and arrange the melon balls on top. Decorate with the mint leaves and chill for several hours.

COOK'S TIP: In this recipe I have used mango purée, which is sold in Indian grocery stores. I like to use Indian mango purée because it is made of a special variety of fruit known as "Alphonso." It has a rich yellow color and a distinctive flavor. Alternatively, purée drained, canned or prepared fresh mango in a blender or food processor and sweeten the purée to taste with confectioner's sugar.

Prune and Banana Dessert
Alubukhara aur Keley ka Mitha

SERVINGS: 4
PREPARATION TIME: 15 minutes
COOKING TIME: 15–20 minutes
PER SERVING: Calories: 240; Fat: 7 g.; Saturated fat: 2.5 g.

Dried prunes and bananas are a healthy combination in this quick-and-easy dessert, which can be served on its own or with low-fat sour cream drizzled with runny honey.

4	firm, ripe bananas, thickly sliced
1 tablespoon	coconut
4½ oz.	stoned ready-to-eat dried prunes
	finely grated rind and juice of 1 lime
	juice of 1 orange
1	star anise
1 oz.	dark soft brown sugar
1 oz.	pecan nuts or walnut halves
1 tablespoon	brandy or dark rum (optional)

→ Preheat the oven to 325°F.
→ Put the bananas in an ovenproof dish and sprinkle the coconut over them. Add the prunes, followed by the lime rind and juice, and orange juice. Mix gently with a metal spoon and bury the star anise under the bananas in the center of the dish.
→ Sprinkle the sugar over the fruit and arrange the nuts on top. Cook for 15–20 minutes.
→ Remove from the oven and allow to cool for 10–12 minutes, then gently stir in the brandy or rum (if using). Serve at room temperature.

Healthy Hint

Bananas are easily digested and a good source of potassium.
Prunes also provide potassium as well as fiber and iron.
Prunes are well known as a remedy for constipation.

Papaya Dessert
Papita ka Mitha

SERVINGS: 4
PREPARATION TIME: 20 minutes, plus cooling and chilling
COOKING TIME: 5 minutes
PER SERVING: Calories: 150; Fat: 0.5 g.; Saturated fat: 0.13 g.

Sweet and succulent golden papaya on raspberry-red sauce, decorated with emerald-green mint, looks absolutely spectacular and let me assure you that this dessert tastes every bit as good as it looks.

1 lb., 2 oz.	raspberries
2-inch piece	cinnamon stick, halved
2–4 oz.	light soft brown sugar
1½ tablespoons	arrowroot
1 tablespoon	brandy (optional)
2	large ripe papayas
a few	fresh mint leaves to decorate

→ Purée the raspberries in a blender and press the purée through a sieve into a saucepan. Add the cinnamon and sugar, then place over low heat. Bring to simmering point, but do not boil.

→ Blend the arrowroot to a smooth paste with a little cold water and stir into the fruit purée. Cook gently, stirring all the time, until the sauce thickens. Remove from the heat and set aside to cool, then stir in the brandy (if using).

→ Meanwhile, halve the papaya lengthwise and remove the seeds. Scrape off the white membrane next to the flesh. It is easier to do this with a grapefruit spoon, which has a serrated edge. Peel the papaya and cut it into bite-sized pieces, then pile them on a serving dish.

→ Remove the cinnamon from the sauce then drizzle some of the sauce over the papaya. Pour some sauce around the edge of the fruit to form a border.

✦ Chill the dessert and remaining sauce for several hours before serving, offering the remaining sauce separately. Decorate with mint leaves.

COOK'S TIP: Papaya seeds have a peppery taste. They can be dried and used along with one or two other whole spices, such as cumin and mustard seeds, as a seasoning cooked in hot oil for vegetables and lentils. You'll find arrowroot in health food stores, larger supermarkets, and Asian stores.

Pineapple and Fig Dessert
Ananas aur Anjeer ka Mitha

SERVINGS: 4–5
PREPARATION TIME: 20 minutes, plus cooling and chilling
COOKING TIME: 10–12 minutes
PER SERVING: Calories: 130; Fat: 0.4 g.; Saturated fat: 0.05 g.

*F*resh, sweet pineapple is heavenly flavored with star anise and cinnamon. Look for golden-skinned, ripe pineapple, which will taste sweet: if you cannot find really sweet fruit, adjust the quantity of sugar to taste. Fresh figs make this dessert look exotic, but other fruits can be used, such as kiwi and/or large strawberries cut into quarters. Dried figs can also be used.

1	large extra-sweet pineapple
2–3 oz.	dark soft brown sugar
2	star anise
2-inch piece	cinnamon stick, halved
2 teaspoons	arrowroot
1 tablespoon	crème de menthe or a few fresh mint leaves
4	fresh figs, quartered

→ Quarter the pineapple lengthwise and peel it with a sharp knife. Use a small, sharp knife to remove the spines or eyes. Cut the flesh into bite-sized pieces and place them in a serving dish.

→ Put the sugar, star anise, and cinnamon in a small saucepan and add 10 fl. oz. water. Bring to a boil and reduce the heat to low. Continue to cook, uncovered, for 8–10 minutes.

→ Blend the arrowroot with a little water and stir it into the syrup. Cook, stirring, until the syrup has thickened slightly. Remove the cinnamon and pour the hot syrup over the pineapple. Place the star anise on top and set aside to cool, then chill for several hours.

➤ Just before serving the dessert, sprinkle the crème de menthe over the pineapple or decorate with the mint leaves, then arrange the figs on top.

 COOK'S TIP: For convenience, use canned pineapple in natural juice. You'll find whole star anise in some larger supermarkets and Asian grocery stores.

Healthy Hint
Fresh pineapple is a good source of vitamin C.
Figs, both fresh and dry, provide calcium, iron,
and potassium, as well as fiber.

Spiced Pears
Masaledar Nashpati

Servings: 6
Preparation time: 10 minutes
Cooking time: 20 minutes, plus chilling
Per serving: Calories: 200; Fat: 3 g.; Saturated fat: 1.8 g.

Serve these lightly spiced pears poached in cider for a refreshing finish to a spicy meal. *Rooh afza,* a concentrated rose-flavored syrup, is mixed with plain low-fat sour cream to serve with the pears. Although you will need to make a trip to an Indian store to buy it, once you have rooh afza, you will find all sorts of different uses for it—it is great for flavoring ice cream, crème fraîche, milkshakes, and yogurt. Rooh afza is also known as the summer drink of the east: to make a non-alcoholic drink, simply dilute it to taste and serve in tall glasses over crushed ice.

6	firm Bartlett pears
1 pint	dry cider
3-inch piece	cinnamon stick, halved
2	star anise
4 tablespoons	sugar
8½ oz.	low-fat sour cream
2 tablespoons	rooh afza or 3 tablespoons rose-flavored syrup
a few	crystallized rose petals, to decorate (optional)

→ Peel, quarter, and core the pears. Put them in a saucepan and add the remaining ingredients, except the sour cream and *rooh afza*. Cover and simmer gently until the pears are *al dente* (tender but firm).

→ Use a draining spoon to transfer the pears to a dish. Strain the syrup into a small saucepan and boil until it is reduced to about 3 tablespoons. Spoon it over the pears and allow to cool, then chill for 2 hours.

→ Mix the sour cream and *rooh afza* together and spoon into a small serving dish so that diners can help themselves.

→ Arrange the pears in individual serving dishes and decorate with rose petals if wished.

COOK'S TIP: To make crystallized rose petals, choose a rose in your favorite color and remove a few petals. Wash and dry the petals, then place them on a sheet of greaseproof paper and brush them lightly with beaten egg white. Sprinkle confectioner's sugar on them and leave to dry completely. If you are worried about using raw egg, use the rose petals without crystallizing. They will look just as attractive.

Rose-Flavored Iced Dessert

GULAB KI KULFI

SERVINGS: 6–8
PREPARATION TIME: 5 minutes, plus cooling and freezing
COOKING TIME: 12–15 minutes
PER SERVING: Calories: 330; Fat: 21.5 g.; Saturated fat: 13 g.

*K*ulfi was introduced to the Indian cuisine by the Moguls. This frozen dessert has a denser texture than the average ice cream and is set in small conical-shaped metal molds. Traditionally, full-cream milk is simmered gently until it is reduced by half, but I have used low-fat milk with low-fat evaporated milk and fat-free half-and-half instead. Rose-flavored syrup is sold by Indian grocers and it adds an exotic scent as well as color to the dessert.

10 fl. oz.	2% milk
14 oz.	canned reduced-fat evaporated milk
10 fl. oz.	fat-free half-and-half
3½–4½ oz.	confectioner's sugar
2–3 tablespoons	rooh afza or rose-flavored syrup
a few	fresh rose petals to decorate

→ Lightly grease a heavy nonstick saucepan (this will prevent the milk from sticking to the pan) and pour in the milk, evaporated milk, and half-and-half. Add the sugar and bring to a boil over medium heat, stirring frequently.

→ Reduce the heat to low and continue to cook for 8–10 minutes, stirring regularly. Remove from the heat and stir in the *rooh afza* or rose-flavored syrup. Allow to cool, stirring occasionally to prevent a skin from forming on top.

→ Pour the mixture into 6 to 8 molds and freeze for 5–6 hours or until firm.

→ To unmold the desserts, hold a mold upside-down under cold running water for 20–25 seconds, taking care not to allow water into the frozen mixture. Quickly dry the outside of the mold with a dishtowel and hold it between the palms of your hands for a few seconds. Then invert the mold on to a plate and lift it off the kulfi. Repeat with the remaining desserts.

✦ Decorate the desserts with rose petals. Serve the kulfi on its own or offer half portions with fresh fruit to reduce the overall fat content of the dessert.

COOK'S TIP: Conical kulfi molds are available in plastic as well as metal from Indian stores. Alternatively, you could use frozen-ice-pop molds.

Yogurt Dessert
SHRIKAND

SERVINGS: 4–5
PREPARATION TIME: 10 minutes, plus draining and chilling
PER SERVING: Calories: 274; Fat: 19.6 g.; Saturated fat: 11.2 g.

*S*hrikand originated in the state of Maharashtra in western India, of which Bombay is the capital. It is one of the easiest, simplest, and most delicious desserts you can make. The yogurt is drained through muslin for several hours, by which time it has a consistency similar to cream cheese. Although the modified yogurt in this recipe has already been strained, it still contains some water, which has to be removed. Traditionally, the dessert is flavored with saffron and cardamom, but I like to use saffron and rose water or rose essence.

30 oz.	modified low-fat plain yogurt (see page 10)
pinch	saffron threads, pounded
2 tablespoons	hot milk
1–2 oz.	confectioner's sugar or to taste
3–4 drops	rose essence or 2 tablespoons rose water

Serve with . . .
fresh fruit, such as blueberries, red currants, kiwi fruit, and strawberries.

→ Line a bowl with a large square of muslin or fine cheesecloth and spoon the yogurt into it. Bring the corners together and tie them so that the yogurt is held in the middle.
→ Put the cloth containing the yogurt into a sieve or colander over a bowl and chill for 4–5 hours or until the whey is removed. (Seasoned with a little salt and pepper or sweetened to taste and chilled, the whey makes a delicious and healthy drink.)
→ Soak the saffron in the hot milk for 20 minutes. Turn the strained yogurt out of the cloth into a large mixing bowl. Add the saffron and beat the yogurt until smooth.
→ Add the sugar and rose essence or rose water, mix thoroughly, and chill for several hours.
→ Serve the dessert in individual stemmed glasses and decorate with fresh fruit.

Spice Suppliers

MANY OF THE spices that we mention in this book are available at Indian grocery stores and larger supermarkets. If you're having trouble finding these aromatic spices near you, however, please contact the following companies:

KALUSTYANS
123 LEXINGTON AVENUE
NEW YORK, NY 10016
212-685-3451

SHALIMAR FOOD AND SPICES
571 MASSACHUSETTS AVE.
BOSTON, MA 02139
617-868-8311
WWW.KASHMIRSPICES.COM

SPICE HOUSE
99 1ST AVE.
NEW YORK, NY 10003
212-387-7812
212-475-4144

SPICELAND, INC.
P.O. Box 34378
CHICAGO, IL 60634-0378
800-FLAVOR-1 OR 800-352-8671 (TOLL FREE)
773-736-1035

THE GREAT AMERICAN SPICE CO.
P.O. Box 80068
FORT WAYNE, IN 46898
888-502-8058 (TOLL FREE)
219-749-8835
WWW.AMERICANSPICE.COM

WEST POINT MARKET
1711 WEST MARKET STREET
AKRON, OH 44313
800-838-2156 (TOLL-FREE)
330-864-2151
WWW.WESTPOINTMARKET.COM

Acknowledgments

I AM GRATEFUL TO Reader's Digest for their fascinating book, *Foods that Harm, Foods that Heal*, which helped me to discover the benefits of many ingredients used in this book. I'm also indebted to K. T. Achaya for his excellent book, *Indian Food— A Historical Companion*. Many thanks to Magimix for supplying gadgets, and to Total Greek Yogurt Company for supplying samples. I'd also like to thank the Solo Sea Salt Company for sending samples, which made me realize that low-sodium salt doesn't hinder flavor. I offer a special thanks to my daughter, Maneesha, for her proofreading help. And finally, I'd like to acknowledge Alan Brooke at Metro Publishing for his faith in this book and the encouragement he offered me.

Index

C

cabbage
  and ginger, 206
  leaf-wrapped fish, 68–69
  pork kebabs, 42
  salad, 230
canapés
  cottage cheese, 44
  spiced potato, 45
canned food, 13
cardamom, 8, 26
carrots
  dry-spiced, and peas, 207
  and green beans with poppy seeds, 204–5
carum (aniseed), 7
cauliflower with green chutney, 208–9
chaat masala, 8
channa dhal (yellow split peas), 12
chapati flour, 7, 12
chapatis, 188–89
  spiced, 190–91
cheese
  chickpeas with Indian cheese, 151–52
  cottage cheese canapés, 44
  kebabs, Indian, 40–41
  paneer, 11
  as protein source, 146
chicken
  in apricot juice, 84–85
  baked, 106–7
  chili, 94–95
  with chili and lime, 88–89
  in coconut milk, 86–87
  cooking hints for, 75–76
  do-piaza, 92–93
  drumsticks, dry-spiced, 96–97
  in green sauce, 98–99
  kebabs, silky, 36–37
  korma, 90–91
  in lentil sauce, 77–79
  meatballs in a rich sauce, 100–1
  meatballs with pilau rice, 180–81
  in milk, 82–83

  pilau, 178–79
  semi-tandoori, 110–11
  spicy roast, 108–9
  tandoori, 32–33
  tikka, 34–35
  tikka masala, 104–5
  in tomato and coconut sauce, 102–3
  in yogurt, 80–81
chickpea flour, 10
chickpeas
  with Indian cheese, 151–52
  in tomato sauce, 149–50
chili chicken, 94–95
chilies, 8–9, 14
choley-paneer (chickpeas with Indian cheese),
  151–52
chukander ka raita (beet raita), 224
chutney
  almond, 225
  date and raisin, 226
  fresh tomato, 227
  green, 208–9
cilantro, 9, 14, 22
cinnamon, 9, 26
cinnamon rice, 175
cloves, 9, 26
coconut
  about, 9
  fat content of, 3
  leeks with, 214–15
  and tomato sauce, 102–3
coconut milk
  chicken in, 86–87
  lamb in, 126–27
cod
  baked, 56–57
  fish in mustard sauce, 64–65
cooking hints, 4
coriander sauce, 66–67
coriander seeds, 9, 22
corn-on-the-cob, spiced, 46
cottage cheese canapés, 44
cucumber and peanut salad, 231
cumin, 9, 21